Chichester
Remembered

Crowds gather in Chichester for the proclamation of Queen Elizabeth II, on 8 February 1952.

Chichester Remembered

Phil Hewitt

Published in association with
Chichester Observer Series

Phillimore

2004

Published by
PHILLIMORE & CO. LTD,
Shopwyke Manor Barn, Chichester, West Sussex, England

ISBN 1 86077 229 3

Printed and bound in Great Britain by
MPG BOOKS LTD
Bodmin, Cornwall

CONTENTS

Acknowledgements ix

Introduction xi

Chapter One: The Great War and Chichester 1

Silent Prayer as Soldier's Son keeps a 70-Year-Old Promise 1

Survivor of the Worst Day in British Military History 3

Carnage at the Somme 4

Survivor of the Horror that never ends 6

Off to War ... on a Bike 7

Childhood during The Great War 9

A World without War 10

'Speedily the Citizens were putting out the Flags' 12

In the Shadow of War 14

Schoolboy's Great War Tribute 15

Chapter Two: Country Life between the Wars 17

Memories of Life down on the Farm 17

A Chronicle of Change 18

Mystery of the Kind Stranger 20

Life at the House 21

Thrashings and Fried Mice 22

Snapshots of Pre-War Life in Selsey 23

Meat is Fresh ... from the Garden Slaughterhouse 25

Photo brings back Flood of Memories 26

Secrets from Harry's Album 27

Chapter Three: The Second World War comes to Chichester 29

Bomb wiped out Three Generations 29

The Day the Bombs fell 31

'Boy' – Victim of the Petworth Bombing 32

Cathedral suffered a Near Miss 34

Those Nights with no Light 35

Stuka Terror hits Sussex 36

City's Wartime 'Mum in a Million'............................ 38
Crash fuels Old Memories 39
Saved by Trees as Bomber crashed 40
'Teddy' Remembers... 41

Chapter Four: The Children of the Second World War 43

The Dogfight Dangers 43
Memories of a Wartime Education 44
Sharing with the Evacuees 46
No Mod Cons for Kate and her Nine Healthy Children 47
For some Evacuees the Real Hardship came after the War....... 48
Evacuee's Fond Memories of Chichester....................... 49
Taste of Awful School Dinners lingers on.................... 50
Rebel with White Drawers.................................... 51
Whatever happened to the Boys From the Class of 45?......... 52
Children's Home Heartbreak.................................. 54
My Childhood Chums – the German POWs........................ 55

Chapter Five: Work in the New Era of Peace................... 57

The Man who taught the Duke to drive........................ 57
The Days when only Posh People had Cars..................... 59
Force was with Archie 60
Company Boss started at Bottom when he was Eight............ 62
No Regrets about a Life spent working with Wood 64
The 'Unseen City' beneath our Feet 65
Alf's Crowning Glory 66
Royal Seal of Approval 67
Door-to-Door for 38 Years................................... 69

Chapter Six: Schooling in the Post-War World................. 71

Sunday School Fun at Portfield Hall......................... 71
Memories of Old-Style Nursery School........................ 71
School's Legacy lives on 300 Years later.................... 73
Knickers, Peaches and Life in a Fifties' Girls School 74
Do the Boys from the Class of '61 still dress like Elvis? ... 75
Alan cherishes Life through a Lens.......................... 76
How Terry and Erica went down the Aisle with Miss Davies 78
Class of '69 was the Last 80

Chapter Seven: Youth comes of Age 81

Happy City Childhood Days 81

Days of Innocence and Rock 'n' Roll 82
Home after 40 Years 83
Liberating Times after Dreary Era 84
Grahame, Tony, Gary ... the Object! 85
If you're going to Tangmere Airfield 87
The Day a Rolling Stone Dropped in for Tea 88
Life-Changing Moment leads to Life in the Theatre 89
Justice at last for the Nearly Man 92

Chapter Eight: Entertainment 93

Fame beckoned as an Ovaltiney 93
Joan: a Friend to the Young Picture-Goers 94
Days of Long Queues and Sticky Pennies! 96
On the Look-Out for Faint Cinema Fans 96
Where there's Brass, there's Music
   – as Horn Player Eric will tell you 99
Longevity is the Spice of Life 100
It's the WOADS without end 102
The Lost Art of Laughter in the Roar 104
Such Happy Memories of Clowning around Archie,
   Bognor's very own Laughing Policeman 105
Folk Song Club – One of the Great Survivors 107

Chapter Nine: A New Theatre is Born 109

Building the Dream 109
Getting it off the Ground 110
When 'King' Olivier reigned 112
Home is where the Art is for Michael 114
Magical Days working with Olivier 116
Sir Laurence and the Dirty Nappy 117
Thrilling Theatre Days with Laurence Olivier 118
Memories of the Great and the Good 119
Carping, Coughing and 'Dearest Danski' 120

Chapter Ten: Sporting Feats and Thrills 123

Olympic Hopeful who ran just for Teenage Fun 123
Catching up on Life through Sport 124
Gunners Career, but Mother said 'No' 123
Referee's Proud Record 126
Tears of Pain and Joy 128
Cold War Tensions set aside for 90 Minutes 128

World Cup Madness and Insults from Jagger 130
Bowling to Bradman Exciting? Not really
    – it was just a Job 133
Rescued Papers recall a Cricketing Legend 134
Skills and Thrills of Sporting Glory 135
Boxing Instructor's Legacy lives. 136

Chapter Eleven: Saints, Sinners and Acts of God 137
Worst Blaze since the War 137
The Great Fire of Chichester 138
The Day that West Dean made the
    Front Page of The Daily Mirror. 140
Flood is Nothing New 141
Camaraderie 'in the Bunker' 143
What they said 144
Antique Dealer accused of stealing Crown Jewels 147
Shocking Mystery has never been solved. 147
Crowds came out – whatever the Occasion 150
Piano took a Bit of a Beating on Jubilee Day 150
It's Quality, not Quantity that counts 151
Hospital had no Equipment – and only one Nurse. 152
Molly – and a Life of Building Fences to protect Others 154
Déja vu for New Park Campaigners 155
Bishop Bell: an Inspirational Leader. 157
The Day Gandhi popped in on Chichester and Bognor 158

Index 161

ACKNOWLEDGEMENTS

I am deeply grateful to the people who told me the tales featured in these pages. I have tried to reproduce their stories with the same honesty, directness and immediacy with which they recounted them. Each interviewee had a fascinating tale to tell, and I hope I have done them justice.

Sadly but inevitably, a good number of the people featured in these pages have passed on since their interview was first published. It seems particularly sad that Sussex fast bowler Jack Nye (pages 132-3) did not live to see Sussex County Cricket Club win their first-ever county championship in 2003. My memory of meeting a man who once bowled to Bradman will stay with me for the rest of my days.

On a personal level, I would like to record my sadness at the passing, all too soon, of Dave Turner (pages 50-1). Dave was a lovely man, kind and immensely likeable. He was always helpful and always interesting. I hope he would have enjoyed this book.

I also very much enjoyed meeting Dennis Burgess (pages 151-2), a man who didn't know how to grow old. I got to know him very much towards the end of his life, but his passion for youth work and his love of young people were utterly undimmed.

I met Freda Leggett twice, and both my interviews with her are reproduced here. She was a remarkable lady who brought the past alive. I feel privileged to have met her. Her death, just before the age of 97, makes her final words on page 18 all the more poignant.

In preparing this book for publication, I found myself having to contact once again people I had interviewed years earlier. I was touched at how enthusiastic so many of them were at the idea of a book of my articles, and I was touched at how willing they were to lend me once again their precious photographs. I would like to record my gratitude to each and every one of them.

I would also like to pay tribute to two people not mentioned in this book, two people who took a huge pride in Chichester and in Chichester history. Reg Davis-Poynter and Peter Parish in their different ways helped me to appreciate Chichester both past and present, and I remember them both with great affection. At the *Chichester Observer* office, they are both greatly missed.

On a happier note, I would also like to record my thanks to *Chichester Observer* series executive editor Keith Newbery. It was Keith's idea to introduce a weekly nostalgia page in the *Chichester Observer* in the first place, and I am delighted that he asked me to write it. I also owe him thanks for allowing me to reproduce here my articles from the paper.

My thanks also go to Noel Osborne of Phillimore for being receptive to the idea of bringing some of my nostalgia features together in book form. Peter Cook, at Phillimore, has done a splendid job in combining the text and the photographs so attractively on the pages that follow.

Finally, I owe a huge debt of gratitude to my wife Fiona for her endless patience and support, both during the preparation of the book and during the final proofing. A linguist by training, she has a keen ear for language and a keen eye for my misspellings! Her endurance and encouragement have been utterly invaluable.

I also owe a debt of gratitude to the staff at the West Sussex Record Office, an institution of which Chichester and West Sussex should be proud. The county's archivists are unfailingly supportive and unfailingly helpful. I hope that they too will regard this book as a useful addition to Chichester history.

Every effort has been made to obtain permission from owners of illustrations. The photographs reproduced on pages 12, 13, 15, 134, 152, 153, 159 and 160 are part of the County Record Office collection. I am also grateful to the *Chichester Observer* series for permission to reproduce a number of photographs included in this book.

INTRODUCTION

In early 1993 I was asked to start writing a weekly nostalgia page for the *Chichester Observer*. I was horrified. I hadn't the slightest idea where I would find the material.

More than ten years later, the page is still going strong, and I can honestly say that I have never struggled to fill it. In fact, it's probably the easiest page to fill in the entire newspaper.

Within weeks it had become apparent that the material I needed for the 'Yesteryear' page was all around me. Chichester is not just a beautiful city. It's a fascinating city. And it's a city which inspires huge affection in its citizens. Cicestrians like nothing better than to talk about Chichester. And that, for me, was a godsend.

The result has been a kind of paper-chase. Always one article leads to the next. Mention a certain cinema one week, and someone will want to reminisce about another the next. Mention a particular war-time incident one week, and the next you'll almost certainly find someone wanting to offer a different perspective.

It was soon clear that my role was to be simply the scribe. It wasn't for me to dictate what I wanted to write about. My nostalgia page – initially called 'Yesteryear' and then renamed 'Remember When' seven years ago – is people power in action. Just as the *Observer*'s letters page is a blank page for the readers, so too is the 'Remember When' page. Readers fill it by telling me about themselves and about the Chichester area.

With time what started to emerge was a composite picture of Chichester and its surrounding villages and countryside in the 20th century. That's when the idea for this book began to take shape. It dawned on me that it was perfectly possible to arrange my 'Remember When' articles into a coherent journey through a turbulent century – a century which brought change at a blistering pace and yet in so many ways contrived to leave Chichester essentially unchanged.

In this book, I have brought together about a hundred of my nostalgia articles in broadly chronological order, from the First World War through to the Second; from country life to town life; from the days when children were seen but not heard through to the days when youth exploded in a new era of empowerment which seemed to lay the world at young people's feet.

The book tells of cinema and amateur dramatics. It also tells of the heady excitement which marked the launch of Chichester Festival Theatre. Also told are tales of sporting prowess in an age of post-war liberation.

The final chapter brings the book to a close with a look at the darker side of Chichester in the 20th century. Significant fires are recalled. So too is the flooding which brought Chichester to the brink of disaster. Also recalled is the Chichester schoolgirl who died at the hands of a brutal killer 80 years ago. Her murder was never solved.

These pages are not history in the strict academic sense. But they are history in an equally valid social sense. They are a mixture of anecdote and journalism, and therein lies their value. Through these pages I hope you will get a sense of what it was to be alive in Chichester in the 20th century. Despite world wars and massive expansion, Chichester emerged from the century with its integrity intact. This book tells its story.

PHIL HEWITT
[November 2004]

The date at the end of each article is the date on which it was published in the *Chichester Observer*.

Chapter One

THE GREAT WAR AND CHICHESTER

Silent Prayer as Soldier's Son keeps a 70-Year-Old Promise

Buttoned up against the bitter November wind, 83-year-old James Lyddall touched the letters which spelt out his father's name.

He then knelt in silent prayer. A 70-year-old promise had finally been kept.

James Lyddall, who fought the Second World War with the Royal Sussex Regiment, had at last honoured the memory of his father Herbert, who perished in the First.

Herbert's name lives on in ten letters on the memorial to the men who died in the battle of Cambrai, a battle which went down in history as one of the bitterest disappointments of the First World War and gave its name to a Chichester street.

The memorial stands stark and cold, just off the infamous Bapaume road. Around it stretch the killing fields of 1914-18.

Lance Corporal Herbert Percy Sydney Lyddall was just 28 when he fell in action on 25 November 1917, leaving behind him a widow and five children in Chichester. Last week, his son James became the first family member to visit the Cambrai memorial in a trip he feared he would never make.

Mr Lyddall was just an infant when his mother, in her grief, gathered her children around her and said she wanted to believe that one day one of them would make a pilgrimage to France in her husband's memory.

In 1993, more than 70 years later, and fearing his own death was not far away, Mr Lyddall returned from Ireland to Chichester to start planning his expedition. But at every turn he met with frustration until the *Chichester Observer* joined forces with P&O Ferries to help him realise his one final wish in life.

Mr Lyddall said the moment was marvellous.

'I told myself I was going to have a prayer there and that's what I did. It was a prayer for my father who was killed. It was also a prayer on my mother's behalf. She never married again. My father was the one love of her life. I said a prayer for the two of them.'

Mr Lyddall was born in Belfast in 1912. Within a couple of years, his family had moved to Chichester where his father signed up with the Royal Sussex Regiment. Just a couple of years after that, his father was dead. 'Before he left England to go out to France, he caught enteric fever. He could have got himself off the draft, but he shrugged it off and wanted to go.'

Mr Lyddall was too young to remember his father. All he knows is the heartache his death brought. 'He was reported missing. Mother got

James Lyddall kneels in prayer as he fulfills a 70-year-old promise.

a telegraph to say they didn't know what had happened to him. Then in the end they must have found his identification because we were told that he was killed in action.'

The family moved back to Ireland soon after the tragic confirmation. Mrs Lyddall needed the support of her own family. But her husband's name was never far from her lips. Mr Lyddall remembers that she spoke of him often.'I think at last she realised that there was no hope left, that he wouldn't ever be coming back. The authorities told her that his name was on the Cambrai memorial and that's when she asked us if we could manage to get to France for her somehow.'

Mr Lyddall came back to Chichester in 1939 to follow in his father's footsteps by signing up with the Royal Sussex Regiment for the Second World War. But after 1945, he returned to Ireland where he remained until two and a half years ago when he decided that Chichester had to be his starting point if he was ever to make his visit to the country where his father died. He came in the hope that his father's name would be on the city's war memorial. He discovered that it wasn't and his determination to get to France grew all the stronger.

Mr Lyddall felt he was making headway, but then this summer he received the bitter news that the Ministry of Defence wouldn't fund his trip because money was available only for widows, not sons. 'I was beginning to think that I would never get there, and now it's solely because of *The Observer* and P&O that I have made it. I feel I can rest now.'

• The tank surprise at Cambrai and the ten days which followed it have been described as 'perhaps the most dramatic of all episodes in the [First] World War'. Historian Liddell Hart, writing just 13 years later, called it 'a sombre sunset after a brilliant sunrise'.

On 20 November 1917, 381 tanks went forward in massed formation without any preliminary bombardment. They crossed all three German lines and advanced five miles, creating a hole in German defences four miles wide. Historian A.J.P. Taylor notes: 'This was a greater success than anything achieved on the Somme or in Flanders and at trifling cost – 1,500 British losses against 10,000 German prisoners and 200 guns.

Over in London church bells were rung, for the only time in the war, to celebrate the victory.'

But no one knew how to use it, and potential triumph rapidly soured in the familiar pattern of despair following hope. The infantry could not keep up with the guns, and the cavalry was easily destroyed. Ten days later, the Germans had recovered the lost ground and a little bit more.

[7 December 1995]

Survivor of the Worst Day in British Military History

The First of July 1996 sees the 80th anniversary of the blackest day in British military history. On the first day of the Somme offensive of the First World War, the British armies suffered a staggering 60,000 casualties. Over the next few months, the casualties mounted until there was barely a family in the country which wasn't touched by grief. Wave after wave of infantrymen was mown down as the heavily-laden soldiers walked slowly into the Germans' deadly machine-gun fire in a terrain mostly bereft of cover. Thousands died instantly, but thousands more writhed in the agony of their wounds on the open battlefield. Long hours in the summer sun elapsed before any attempt could be made to retrieve them.

Chichester man Arthur Fisher was there, and in a sense he was one of the lucky ones. His war was short, but it ended in capture, not death.

His daughter Gladys Willard, of Melbourne Road, Chichester, was born three years after Arthur's return from two years' forced labour down the mines in Germany. 'I don't know where exactly the mines were, but I believe the conditions were fairly bad', she says. 'In the mines he had to crawl on his hands and knees. At one point when he missed the lift down the mineshaft, he was forced to stand still for hours on end. If he moved, he would be hit with a gun.'

Arthur Fisher and his comrades in No.1 Platoon 'B' Company 8th Sussex Home Guard, in the Second World War.

CHICHESTER PHOTOGRAPHIC SERVICE LTD.

No. 1 PLATOON "B" COY. 8TH SUSSEX HOME GUARD

Back Row—PTE. CHITTY (M.), PTE. HAWKINS, PTE. FISHER (L.), PTE. CLEMENTS, PTE. OLIVER, PTE. HORNE, PTE. FISHER (A.), PTE. SPEARMAN, PTE. SUTER, L/CPL. CHITTY (R.).

Front Row—L/CPL. CLIFFORD, PTE. SAMWAYS, PTE. BROWN, PTE. BARNES (S.), CPL. JOYCE, SGT. BEAGLEY, LIEUT. MATTHEWS, SGT. SCAMMELS, CPL. WINGATE, L/CPL. MITCHEL, PTE. BARNES (J.), PTE. MESSINGHAM, CAPT. HARVEY.

Arthur, who was born in Rogate, and his three brothers, who also served in 1914-18, survived the war, but Mrs Willard recalls that the war wasn't a subject they liked to dwell on.

Her knowledge of his service is sketchy. Like countless others, Arthur lied about his age when he took the King's shilling at Chichester barracks. He was just seventeen and a half when he signed up. Arthur spent a couple of weeks in training and then, apparently, he was switched from the Royal Sussex to the North Staffs where there were more gaps to be filled.

Within days he was in action. Mrs Willard doesn't know at what point he joined the horror of the Somme. All she knows is that he was very quickly captured.

'It was just me and my sister, and neither of us knew much about what he went through. He came home as soon as he was allowed home in 1918 and he got married in 1920. I was born in 1921.'

For much of his life, Arthur, who died 15 years ago aged 83, was a cattleman, but when the Second World War dawned he was keen to serve his country once again.

He joined the Local Defence Volunteers and became a Home Guard, Mrs Willard recalls. 'We lived at Merston. He used to do his duties at Merston. They used to go to a little hut beside Merston church, but what he did I don't really know. We used to say 'What have you been doing, dad?' and he used to say 'Keeping watch, keeping watch'.

'As long as they were involved, it did them a lot of good. A lot of them must have been 1914 men. He wanted to be involved. He wanted to do fire-watching but having to get up at four in the morning to milk the cows, he just couldn't do it as well. But he was in the Home Guard right to the end. He was so proud of the brass badge he had on his uniform.'

[13 June 1996]

Arthur Fisher ... proud to be in the Home Guard.

Carnage at the Somme

77 years ago today, thousands of British soldiers went over the top to join the bloodbath on the Somme. A couple of days later, they were joined by Sergeant Charles Tulett, one of the 12 young men on the staff of Shippam's in Chichester to join up just after the First World War broke out in August 1914.

Sgt Tulett, who lived in Grove Road, served with D Company of the 7th (Service) Battalion of the Royal Sussex Regiment, the first of the new Kitchener Battalions raised in the county. He went over to France on 31 May 1915 and served throughout the war on the Western Front, receiving the Military Medal for his gallant conduct.

Towards the end of his life he twice contributed articles to the *Chichester Observer*, and in 1982, in his 93rd year, he was encouraged by regimental historians to commit his memoirs to paper. A copy of his 36-page manuscript is now kept in the regimental archives in Chichester, a testimony to a remarkable man who died in March 1983. The manuscript makes compelling reading – a Chichester man's first-hand experience of First World War carnage.

Sgt Tulett joined the fighting on the Somme for the attack on enemy trenches at Ovillers on 7 July 1916.

Charles Tulett in full kit outside Shippam's, just about to go back to France after five days' leave.

Charles Tulett convalesces in Kent after being wounded on the Somme in 1916.

'Undaunted by the frightful casualties suffered in action the preceding days', he wrote, 'we were on our toes, knowing full well a whole brigade and two divisions had failed …

'Five lines of German trenches were included as objectives, the farthest being just east of Ovillers church which meant crossing 400 yards of no man's land and penetrating 1,200 yards into the German trench system.

'At 6.45am on July 7 intensive bombardment of our guns began, and later the German artillery started on our trenches, causing heavy casualties. On the evening before the attack I was detailed to go down to the transport to collect a draft of 16 men, mostly youngsters about 16 or 17 years of age.

'Of these we had four in our platoon, pitched straight into battle, and over the top we went only to be met by artillery fire, and a very heavy barrage of machine-gun fire causing terrible casualties.

'I had gone about ten yards when a shell exploded quite close to me, burying me up to my shoulders, also killing many of those poor kids. Luckily some of the lads dug me out, very shaken and shocked, but more was to come as when I had gone a few more yards I had a bullet through my tin helmet, taking a small piece out of my ear and a hole at the back of the helmet the size of the palm of your hand, a very lucky escape.

'But I still went on as many poor chaps were being bowled over like ninepins, and to see the dead and dying, hearing the cries of the wounded, was terrifying.

'However I still struggled on, and most of the troops who were fortunate to do so had reached the German lines, but now had come to some of the Kaiser's crack troops, engaged for a while in hand-to-hand fighting.

'I shot one, but at that moment I received a bullet through my right wrist, causing me terrible pain, but managed to get to the trench which was full of both English and mostly German dead.'

No attempt could be made to get the wounded back to their own lines until darkness fell. Tulett took with him a lad of 17 who had been shot in the shoulder.

'We started to go over in pitch darkness, mostly on our knees and stomach as it was very dangerous to take risks standing up, and we never knew actually where we were, but occasionally flares would go up, lighting up no man's land, and the sight that met our eyes, the dead, the cries of the wounded, and to think you couldn't help them, was terrible.' Sgt Tulett's wound took him back to England, but his young companion perished, despite Tulett's best efforts.

In April 1917 Sgt Tulett again showed courage in adversity. He was awarded the Military Medal for his bravery on patrol and his part in the release of a number of Royal Fusiliers taken prisoner at Monchy.

In fact, during the fighting at Arras and Monchy he received no fewer than four certificates for gallant conduct and bravery in the field.

He was recommended for a commission, but the end of hostilities on 11 November 1918 put this into abeyance. He greeted the armistice with inevitable relief.

'There is one memory that I shall always remember. On leaving the trenches (near St Amand) we passed through a small French village where there was a small group of elderly men and women who came running over to us, hugging and kissing us, with tears in their eyes, so pleased to think it was all over, a very emotional occasion for many of us, one I shall never forget.'

Sgt Tulett returned to Shippam's, who had paid his parents ten shillings a week throughout the war. Tulett went on to complete 47 years' service with the food company, retiring as foreman in 1955.

Sgt Tulett's son Victor, aged 71, recalls him as 'a marvellous old boy', a brave and distinguished man who displayed remarkable courage amid the terrible ordeals of trench warfare. Victor, who lives in Chichester, said: 'As youngsters we used to sit and listen to his stories in winter evenings, but at the time, we just didn't realise what he went through. It was just carnage. No one can realise what these poor devils suffered. I went through World War Two, but we had nothing like what they went through. Everybody should be appreciative of what these soldiers did in the 1914-1918 war. We have got our freedom thanks to them.'

[1 July 1993]

Charles Tulett pictured at Shippam's in the year of his retirement, 1955.

Survivor of the Horror that never ends

Joan Burchell's father survived the horrors of the First World War – but at a price he continued to pay until his dying day 50 years later.

Midhurst man Wyndham Burchell lived to the age of 82, but he never regained the sight he lost in a mustard gas attack during the muddy bloodbath of Passchendaele in 1917.

Joan, now Mrs Marriner and living in Fishbourne, was born three years after the war to a father who never saw her.

'My father was in the Horse Artillery', she recalls. 'He was blinded by this mustard gas, but he was a super chap. He was in hospital for a long time, but was eventually discharged. His doctor had to go the House of Lords to get him his pension.

'My father was a lovely man in every way. He had a great sense of humour in spite of everything. He was very outgoing and although he was blind, you would never know it if you went into a room and just started speaking to him.'

Wyndham overcame his injuries to the extent that he was able to resume his pre-war job as a gardener for a Mr Manley-Smith near Easebourne. 'The odd thing was that the problems would come back. He was gassed in the November and every year at around about that time he would bubble up in blisters and his eyes always reacted every year right up until he died.'

Her father's disability meant that Joan didn't get out as much as perhaps she might have done, and her mother wasn't one for going out either. That's maybe why she got involved in entertainments, taking part in a string of variety shows with a group of Midhurst children. 'Mrs Stone, who was the Barclay's Bank manager's wife, and

Wyndham Burchell with his grandson Melvyn.

Gunner Wyndham Burchell during the First World War.

Mrs Robertson, who was married to the draper, ran the group that we children belonged to.'

It was in the mid-1930s and Joan reckons she must have been about 12 or 13 years old.

'We used to do these shows every year or so. They were song and dance and poetry and just general entertainment really. We took a different guise and different names each time. The only one I can think of was The Masqueraders. We tried to think that we were somebody different every time. On that occasion we had masks.'

She still remembers the names of many of her comrades on stage. Ian Haslett, Bernard Shearing, Joan Stone, Sydney Fleet and Molly Greenslade are just a few.

Others include Margaret Sears, Marcia Stone, Kathleen Hall and Thelma Lee, plus the Knight twins and Iris Lee. Joan recalls it all as good fun, an attractive alternative to a Midhurst which she remembers as rather dreary. Apart from the concert parties, her pleasures came at the convent where she went to school. 'I enjoyed school. We always did a lot of art and sewing – all sorts of sewing, and we were very good at it. It has stood me in good stead.'

But always the Great War loomed large, an inescapable past. Joan's father embodied the horror his generation had suffered – a horror he hoped no one would suffer again. And every year, as the anniversary of that fateful gas attack approached, the horrors would come back to haunt him...

[September 26 1996]

Off to War ... on a Bike

Off to war on a bike ... It doesn't sound terribly grand, but the role of Lieutenant-Colonel Arthur Tyndale-Biscoe and his colleagues was potentially a vital one.

Lt-Col Tyndale-Biscoe, who lived in Bognor Regis, was in the Territorials when the First World War broke out. His unit was the 9th (Cyclist) Battalion of the Hampshire Regiment, based at the old County Hall in Chichester. Their task was essentially one of patrol, and it was a wide area they covered.

Lt-Col Tyndale-Biscoe's daughter Rosamond Milanes, aged 87, of Bosham, was just two when the war broke out. She has dim memories of the day the war ended, dim memories of rushing out into the streets and celebrating with special sandwiches - anchovy paste, no less.

Her memories of her father, though, are fond and vivid. Lt-Col Tyndale-Biscoe lived to the ripe old age of 96. He died in 1968.

'He was lovely. He was the absolute darlingest man. He was always the same. He never had a bad temper. He was an absolute dear chap.' Born in Oxfordshire, he came to live in Bognor Regis in about 1912 – first in Victoria Drive, then in Gloucester Road, then in Upper Bognor Road. What he did for a living, Mrs Milanes struggles to say. He was what they used to call a country gentleman. 'He never had much money, but he was very clever with money. That's why we could live in a big house, although we didn't have a lot of money.'

Mrs Milanes was too young to remember too much about his First World War bicycling duties, but she knows that he and his comrades

The 9th Hants march through Chichester.

were responsible for a big stretch of coastal England – from Littlehampton down to Selsey, the Isle of Wight and probably as far along the coast as Bournemouth.

She still possesses papers detailing the remit of the battalion's patrols. The official document states: 'The object of a patrol is to prevent an enemy from landing unobserved and unreported. He must watch for anything unusual particularly on the sea or in the sky. He will allow no one to approach without being certain of his identity. He will on no account enter into conversation with any person whatever. On sighting an enemy or any unusual or suspicious thing, the men will do what they can to conceal themselves and observe. As soon as there is anything definite to report, one man should take the information as quickly as possible to the nearest support or coastguard station, and one man should remain to obtain further information.'

Lt-Col Arthur Tyndale-Biscoe instructs his men at Arundel camp.

The instructions also point out that coast patrols should not keep constantly on the move, but should frequently stand still and listen. 'In order to detect any movement of the enemy in the offing they should move in the line from which the sound of the waves on the beach will be least audible.'

Also detailed in the document are practicable landing places – key places for patrols to watch: 'Landing is practicable in moderate weather from Littlehampton to Selsey except just SW of Bognor where the rocks are a source of danger.' The document draws up a list of landing places in order of importance and assesses the obstacles which would face an invader's inland advance.

Good metalled roads are listed, as are positions for opposing the enemy. The disused Arundel canal is a suggestion for one section, while a landing between Littlehampton and Barn Rocks, it suggests, could be opposed in winter from the position along Ryebank Rife.

Even included is a list of privately owned telephones in the area. Pagham sub post office could be reached on Bognor 11, Bognor pier on 77. Clearly the authorities had thought of everything. And in Lt-Col Tyndale-Biscoe they had just the man to lead them …

Fortunately, however, the invasion never came.

[February 18 1999]

Childhood during The Great War

Edith Knights well remembers the day her father came back from the First World War.

Mrs Knights, who now lives opposite the *Chichester Observer* offices, was a ten-year-old in Funtington on the day her daddy returned from five years of fighting.

'I was only five when he left and he was away for years. He ended up in Afghanistan at the end of the war. He was in France for most of it but he never used to talk about it, but I suppose also you don't listen when you're young, and then when they've gone you've got nobody to ask. But I do remember the day he came home. We went down on a horse and trap to meet him at Bosham station. The first thing he said when he came back was "shut the gate", and I thought "oh dear". He was very strict.'

Even so, Mrs Knights, who is now 86, remembers her childhood as a time of almost limitless freedom. 'We were allowed to go into the fields. We used to play in Kingley Vale and we had a lovely time. The farmers never stopped us going into the fields and it was wonderful.'

One particularly fond memory is of the Christmas parties at Funtington Hall, then owned by Major Grills. 'It was a great loss to the village when they went. They were very kind people. We all had a lovely present. I had a little china tea service. It really was beautiful.'

Another character who has stayed in her memory through the decades was Mr Walker, the priest. 'He had three daughters, and all during the war, the first war, we used to go every Saturday afternoon to do needlework. He was always a very nice man. It was one of the old churches, and his daughters used to do a lot of the church work. There was nobody else to do it. 'He was there all the time that I remember, and my grandfather was parish clerk and did everything for the church.'

A young Edith Knights.

By trade, Mrs Knights' grandfather was an undertaker and builder, and Mrs Knights well remembers watching him make the coffins. 'I used to go up to his workshop and watch my grandfather and my uncle working. That's why I don't believe in cremation. They used to go to Covers and get all the wood.'

Mrs Knights didn't see the corpses, but she insists these were days when there was a healthy lack of mystique around the subject of death. 'The bodies would be kept at home for a week. They wouldn't go to chapels of rest like they do now. They would be in the spare room with candles. They used to leave the coffin open and people would come and see them. It was a very natural thing to do.'

As for schooling, Mrs Knights would go to West Ashling where discipline was the order of the day. 'There was a very very hard master, but we were pleased of that because it has taught us to be good citizens. I had the cane every day for talking and disobedience and all the rest of it. I deserved it, I'm sure!' She doesn't recall having any favourite lessons: 'It certainly wasn't maths. I didn't like maths and things like that, I could never get on with it and I still can't.' But among the highlights were the friendships she formed, friendships which have lasted a lifetime. She is still in contact with a school chum now living in Portsmouth.

'We are in contact with one another on the telephone, but I am afraid there are not a lot of us left now.'

[November 2 1995]

Above: *Mr Walker, the nice priest.*

Left: *Pupils at West Ashling school. Mrs Knights is second from right in the middle row.*

A World without War

War? What war? The happy children at Chichester's Bishop Otter College School hardly noticed that the First World War was raging.

Amy Farenden, née Birch, was one of the pupils at the school, which has long since gone. Her father was away at the front, and many of the other children were minus fathers and uncles. 'But we didn't pay very much attention to the war. We were just too young', she recalls.

Mrs Farenden, now 80, remembers fondly the times her father came home on leave, particularly one occasion when the family had moved house in the meantime and laughingly watched dad go to a front door which was no longer his.

But for the most part, the war was not a factor in a world in which Miss Harris, Miss Redman and Miss Funnel were the people who mattered most. The trio were teachers at the school. Miss Harris was a strict disciplinarian who became even stricter when she moved on to the Central School; Miss Redman lived with Miss Harris; and Miss Funnel lived in Spitalfield Lane.

'Miss Harris lived in Westhampnett Road and I used to carry the school books home for her. She rode on one of those upright bicycles. I suppose she was probably in her late 20s or early 30s. As a small girl I didn't really take much notice of people's ages. But it was all such a lovely time. We always had students that were studying to be teachers. My brother and sister were at the school as well. I wore button boots and very often got them on the wrong feet. The teacher had a button hook and she would inspect us when we came in. We would have to change if we got the boots on the wrong way round.'

Another regular feature was hand and nail inspection. Anyone with dirt in their finger nails would be given a sharpened matchstick, and they would know what they had to do.

In some respects, things were rather primitive. The wash room, for instance, centred on a stone sink and a permanently wet floor. There was also a roller towel, and this too was always soaked. As for drinks, water came from a tap over a drain with an enamel mug chained to it.

But there were plenty of pleasures to be had. Near the school was a stream, and nearby was a spring with water gushing out – inevitably a big attraction for the children.

Mrs Farenden recalls: 'I used to love digging around there, and I would have soaking feet and be late for school.'

Another feature, this time terrifying, was the cows waiting nearby for slaughter at the abattoir. 'It was at the bottom of College Lane. There would be cows that would rush out of there. They would know that they were going to be killed. I would scramble up into the hedge crying like fury.'

The children of the First World War at school in Chichester. Mrs Farenden is extreme right in the middle row. Third from right in the back row is the man dubbed 'the father of Chichester archaeology', the late Alec Down, author of a series of authoritative books on Roman Chichester.

11

More cheerful was Christmas when the teacher would ask pupils to bring in dried fruit, sugar and nuts to make a Christmas pudding. 'The teacher would cut the pudding into slices and wrap it in ordinary ruled school paper for us to take a slice home to mother on the day we broke up.'

But Mrs Farenden has a confession to make. 'Mine didn't often get home. It would get nibbled on the way!'

[22 September 1994]

'Speedily the Citizens were putting out the Flags'

Cicestrians, like everyone else, knew that the end of the war was coming in those early days of November 1918.

When it came, the *Chichester Observer* relegated it to page four, reported it with all due sobriety, and reproduced the historic declaration which the Prime Minister made to the House of Commons. 'The Armistice was signed at five o'clock this morning,' he intoned. 'Hostilities ceased on all fronts at 11am today … Thus came to an end the cruellest and most terrible war that has ever scourged mankind. I hope we may say that thus, on this fate-filled morning, came to an end all wars', the Prime Minister somewhat optimistically added. 'With you I rejoice, and thank God for the victories which the Allied Arms have won, bringing hostilities to an end and peace within sight.'

The *Chichester Observer* in its columns sought to catch a flavour of the day. 'The certitude of an armistice and surrender by Germany had put all Cicestrians in a state of joyous expectation', it recorded. 'But many canny ones knowing of premature rejoicing counselled restraint on patriotic fervour until the news of the signing of the armistice was really official.

'It was about 11 o'clock on Monday that telephone messages of the glorious news came through', the *Observer* continued, 'and speedily the citizens were busy in putting out flags, and cyclists and children appeared with miniature flags. It happened to be "Gun Week for War Bonds",

Peace celebrations at Singleton 1919. A community unites in joy.

Peace celebrations at Singleton 1919. The Rev. F.A.G. Leveson-Gower is pictured with children in costume.

and a six-inch British Howitzer, with the boys who had been serving it in France, took up a week's position at the Cross, the centre of all Chichester's public manifestations.

'This helped to attract the crowd, which was joined at noon (the Cathedral's bells a little earlier pealing out the jubilant clangour of victory) by the Deputy Mayor (Alderman Turnbull), the Mayoress (Lady Garland) etc.', the *Observer* added.

'The Deputy Mayor mounting the Howitzer, regretting that the Mayor was still confined at home with bronchial trouble instead of being with them at such an auspicious moment, said the Mayor had received news from the Mayor of Portsmouth that the armistice had been signed at five o'clock that morning.'

The Deputy Mayor told the crowds that the presence of the gun at the Cross reminded them that they still had a duty to do in supporting the Government in meeting its financial responsibilities. But he voiced his confidence that 'Chichester would not be found lacking in its patriotic support of providing silver bullets'.

He hoped Sir Archibald, the Mayor, would make a speedy recovery and lead them in happily celebrating the glorious peace. The Deputy Mayor, in conclusion, paid a tribute to the 'grand work of our Allies in the attainment of victory'.

And then the celebrations began ... and boy, did Chichester have fun. The *Chichester Observer* didn't put the victory on the front page, but the city certainly knew its priorities even if its paper didn't.

The National Anthem was sung, and three cheers heartily given for the Navy, Army, and Allies.

Large crowds promenaded the street all the afternoon and evening when the 'street electric lamps were promptly set giving their pre-war radiance and brightness of illumination'.

At Graylingwell War Hospital, the Commanding Officer, Surgeon-Colonel Kidd, with the Matron, visited every ward to announce the news. Ringing cheers were raised for the King, President Wilson, and the Allies, the ovation for President Wilson including the American wounded in hospital.

Fog signals were let off at the Railway Station at noon by the Stationmaster (Mr H.J.Swan).

Meanwhile, the signing of the armistice with Germany was signalled in 'Happy Bosham' by the pealing of the bells in the parish church. 'Like magic', the *Observer* reported, 'flags appeared from all quarters and fluttered gaily from almost every house before noon on Monday'.

A special service of thanksgiving was quickly convened by the vicar, and 'the joyous bells summoned the thankful villagers to join in praising God for the blessings of a victorious peace'.

At 6.30p.m., the church was packed to its utmost capacity. The service was 'thoroughly congregational' and was 'joined in heartily by the worshippers'.

The atmosphere inspired the *Chichester Observer* reporter to wax distinctly lyrical: 'As the congregation streamed forth from the sacred edifice, from the ancient windows of which once more shone out the light after four years of darkness, the bells burst forth again into a joyous peal.'

[11 November 1993]

In the Shadow of War

January 1920 was a month which saw Chichester still struggling to come to terms with the massive loss of life suffered in the Great War. More than a year had passed since the cessation of hostilities, but still the shadows of war lay over the city.

The month brought the unveiling of the Birdham School war memorial. It is difficult to imagine a more graphic illustration of the sheer scale of death throughout the communities. No fewer than 27 former scholars of the school perished in the war, their names now recorded on the school's solid oak tablet.

The Duke of Richmond and Gordon unveiled the memorial in a ceremony which the *Chichester Observer* confidently predicted would live long in the memory of those who took part in it. 'May the names carved on this tablet, O Saviour, who lovest the obedience of children, inspire all, who shall hereafter be scholars within these walls, manfully to fight under Thy banner and to be Thy faithful soldiers and servants unto their lives' end', the Duke told the gathering. He then went on to voice the very feeling which emerges from even the briefest of glimpses through the *Chichester Observer* of the day.

Although the fighting had come to an end, there was still a great deal of unrest, and it was now the duty of every citizen to rehabilitate the nation, the Duke intoned.

Communities – Selsey and Chichester in particular – were still contemplating what form their war memorials should take.

But there were too many survivors of the war to allow people to look exclusively to the past. The New Year 1920 was seen in with a fancy dress ball, staged in conjunction with the National Federation of Discharged and Demobilised Soldiers and Sailors, an event which brought a large crowd to the Assembly Rooms.

Much the same was happening in Bognor where Colonel Campbell doubled as Father Christmas and where General Forbes declared himself honoured to be the guest of the Comrades of the Great War.

All discharged and demobilised soldiers should join the Comrades Club where they would be sure of a warm welcome and expert advice for the future, the general urged.

There was no doubt that the lot of former heroes was a tough one, and the temptations were often great. A meeting in Chichester in January 1920 was told of the abuses of war pensions that were already beginning to emerge. The finance and general purposes sub-committee of the West Sussex War Pensions heard that some former soldiers were continuing

Chichester Territorials leave for the Front.

to draw treatment allowances despite finding regular work. Others were receiving grants from the King's Fund to buy tools and stock, but then selling the items at a profit. Stern warnings were delivered, but still the overall mood was one of gratitude and appreciation. Chichester's main concern remained how best to accommodate the young men who had given so much.

The month ended with the calling of a public meeting to bring together as many former comrades as possible. The principal aim was to decide on the best way to commemorate the Great War and keep alive the memory of the fallen.

But if you read between the lines, it was also an attempt to keep alive the wartime solidarity of those who lived to come home. The forces of social cohesion were clearly being given a nudge – particularly through the formation of a new body aimed at voicing the concerns of a social class which was feeling distinctly disadvantaged.

Think back to the days of poverty and deprivation which marked the early years of the century, and you might imagine the new group would be advancing the cause of the lower or working classes.

But no. The new group was the Chichester branch of the Middle Classes Union. Mr Crowe, the chairman, said there was no doubt that such a union was badly needed.

[12 January 1995]

Schoolboy's Great War Tribute

A Chichester schoolboy has stood at the First World War graveside of the great great uncle he didn't know he had. Late last month 15-year-old Duncan Tennent, of Chichester Road, West Wittering, set out on a Chichester High School for Boys visit to the battlefields of the Great War.

Two days before he left, he received a surprise package which gave the whole trip an unexpected poignancy. The package, from Duncan's grandfather, contained documents detailing the death in action of his grandfather's uncle, Harold Christopher Bates.

15

A Lieutenant in the Royal Engineers, Bates was killed at Ypres in 1915. Details of his grave allowed the school party to pay their respects in person in a pre-Remembrance Day tribute. Duncan said: 'It was quite remarkable really, especially when you think he was just one of millions. There were World War One cemeteries every few kilometres. There were thousands of graves.'

Bates, who was around 25 years old when he died, worked before the war as a civil engineer for the London, Midland and Scottish Railway. He was a man who inspired great admiration in the short years of his life.

A letter to Bates' parents from his army chaplain, W.J.Torrance, tried to offer comfort. Included in the letter was a flower from one of the wreaths which were placed upon his remains. Torrance wrote: 'Only last Sunday I was privileged to give him Holy Communion in the advanced billet of his Company and with his other Officers and men. We lose a friend, the Army loses a gallant Officer, but he gains the rest and peace of Paradise. HE GAINS, even though it is difficult for the rest of us to look at it in this way.

'I believe that he is the first Officer of our division to have fallen, and I am told by his men that he had already shown unusual courage and sang froid in various perilous undertakings. They speak of him with unqualified admiration and affection.'

Torrance goes on to describe the cemetery, set beneath the shade of a great church, battered and torn by shells. Trees and hedges screen the place and give it an air of peace and rest.

Major Butterworth wrote to the family with details of Bates' last minutes.

'No 3 (Harold's) section were putting up a wire entanglement round a small work called Coloui Post, some little way (150 yards perhaps) behind the firing line. They started work at about 9pm and all went well until 11pm. A few bullets passed from time to time, but it was comparatively quiet.

'Just at 11 a machine gun opened fire from a point to the right of the post, which was replied to by the enemy by heavy machine-gun and rifle fire. A storm of bullets swept over the work, and one of these hit poor Harold in the forehead. He went down without a sound, and death must have been quite (or nearly) instantaneous.'

Comrades dressed the wound and took him with all speed to the first-aid post of the 1st Seaforths.

'Here I found him at midnight with four of his section in attendance. Nothing could be done. We carried him back to the place where the Section Waggons were packed, and then brought him back here. His section behaved splendidly. They all loved him to a man, and his loss to the Section and the Company is greater than I can estimate.

'Personally I mourn for a dear friend, for his lovable disposition, cheerfulness and keenness for his work had endeared him to myself and the entire Company.

'Ever since we came up here and have been under fire, he has been an example to EVERYONE of pluck and general courage. I never saw him once flinch and duck at a bullet, which very few can say at the start.'

[7 November 1996]

Chapter Two

COUNTRY LIFE BETWEEN THE WARS

Memories of Life down on the Farm

Ninety-two-year-old Freda Leggett, of Chichester, grew up the daughter of a West Lavant farmer in the early years of the century. It's a time she remembers with affection.

Above: *Freda Leggett's parents.*

Right: *Charles Harris – a true countryman (c.1929).*

Her father, Charles Harris, worked a busy day, but never complained. The work was back-breaking, but it was a time when people seemed somehow more accepting of their lot, Mrs Leggett believes.

'He started work at 6.30 in the morning and worked until five o'clock at night, six days a week including Saturday. All the workers would go to the farmhouse after five on a Saturday to get their wages. They got 12 shillings and sixpence a week.

'Horses helped with the ploughing, and I can remember them sowing the corn. The corn was raked over by a horse. When the corn grew up ready for harvesting, my dad would go into the field and cut around the field with a scythe, and then the horse would come in.'

The corn would be cut and then put out to dry. The ricks were then thatched to keep the water out. 'In the autumn a threshing machine

17

would come and thresh the corn to be made into flour.'

Mrs Leggett can still recall the straps her father would wear around his legs to keep the mice and rats from running up him. There were no combine-harvesters, and around a dozen men would do the work one machine would do today. 'My father was always a farm worker. I think he did everything on the farm apart from milk cows.'

Mrs Leggett's father came from a family of 13 or 15, as did her mother, but between them they had just two children – Freda and her elder sister who tragically died of Spanish flu in 1918. 'I was in the farmhouse until I got married and then instead of leaving, my dad came to live with us at West Stoke.'

Mrs Leggett was never destined for farm work herself. At the age of 14 she was an apprentice dress-maker with her heart set on becoming a lady's maid. Sadly, her mother's final illness meant that things worked out otherwise.

There were sadnesses in store for her, but unaware of the future, she enjoyed in those early years a childhood spent joyously close to nature. 'My life as a child was lovely. There was great excitement when we found the first primrose or the first violet. You just wouldn't think about it now. And the boys would go out bird-nesting. You wouldn't be allowed to do that now, but they would all go out collecting eggs.'

A family portrait. Back left is Charles Harris; middle right: Freda Leggett; middle left: Freda's husband George.

Church was a fixture of the week – twice a day on a Sunday with Sunday school in between. 'It wasn't a chore. It was just the way we were brought up. If you haven't got faith, then what have you got?' Faith is the cornerstone of her life to this day. It is a source of comfort and the source of her equanimity. 'I am nearing the end of my cycle of life. It doesn't worry me. I am just looking forward to seeing all my family again. I fear the death bed, but I don't fear death itself – not at all. Not at my age.'

[8 October 1998]

A Chronicle of Change

'It's like comparing a rusty old motorbike with Concorde', says Freddie Mansbridge as he looks back at farming methods ancient and modern. Freddie, who lives in Highfield Lane, Oving, has just written his life story, a detailed chronicle of 77 years as a Sussex countryman. Ask him what a countryman is, and he'll tell you straight: it's someone versed in the ways of the country from the moment of birth, someone who spends his boyhood searching for birds' nests, his manhood mastering every job on the farm, and his whole life watching the world change.

Well versed in country ways – Freddie Mansbridge.

Born in Sussex, he went to school in the Pulborough, Petworth, Billingshurst area, before settling at Chilgrove during the war years, a time when he became only the second person in the country to have a combine harvester.

In Freddie's boyhood everything had been done by horse, but by now the pace of change was gathering. 'There have been vast changes. You just can't compare. It is like trying to compare an old motorbike with Concorde, it's so different now to what it was then. Where there were 20 men on a farm, there are now about two, what with all the mechanisation. It was all horses when I first started. There weren't any tractors about. My first tractor that I saw was in 1922.'

He remembers distinctly that it was seen as a threat. 'It was just like secretaries and typewriters, with all the secretaries reckoning their jobs were going to go when typewriters first came out. Everyone thought it was going to do away with their jobs.'

Freddie's response was to learn every farming job that was going. He reckoned it was his best insurance in a changing industry, and to this day he proudly boasts there wasn't a job on a farm he couldn't do. He got his first threshing machine in 1935 just as the steam threshing machines were going out, and he looks back proudly on a lifetime of heavy toil. 'Those were very happy days, the way of life. You were out in the country, and that was where you had to stay.'

As a boy, his wages were 12 shillings and sixpence – 'and this was in old money, before this new-fangled stuff'. It was hardly rich pickings for a summer weekly workload of 56 hours, and 48 in the winter. No wonder he needed a treat at the weekends, and that treat, inevitably, was a trip into Chichester, a city, he says, which has sadly declined since 1931 when he first saw it.

Back in those days there were crowds and crowds, and you would wonder where all the people could possibly have come from. Today it is, in his view, derelict, empty of interest, 'all offices and estate agents now'.

A special place in his memory goes to the war years, a period which he describes as uncanny, though he declines to expand, save to say that his part-time fire service work brought him sights which he never thought he would see and would never want to see again.

Looking back on it all, Freddie says he realised his memories belonged to a way of life which was disappearing forever. Hence the book, a task completed in just a few months at the prompting of a friend who urged him to chronicle a country life which could never again be lived in quite the same way.

Names have been changed in deference to those he knew, but the facts are just as they were, written up by hand in a text which runs to nearly 200 pages. The title is simply *The Life and Times of a Countryman*. What else could it be?

Freddie changes his own name in the book, signing off as Freddie Mans, though few will be deceived. Even fewer will fail to be touched by his unpublished work's closing sentence. 'Well, now I am 77 years young', he writes, 'I think it's nearly time to put my tools away, and make use of that seat in the garden.'

[21 October 1993]

19

Mystery of the Kind Stranger

The childhood mystery of the kind gentleman still haunts 92-year-old Freda Leggett many decades later.

Mrs Leggett's sister Dorothy, who was born in 1901, suffered from polio and was confined to a bath chair. But their mother liked them both to get out and, come Goodwood Week, they would watch the race-goers go by in their horses and traps. 'At Adsdean House in Funtington there were the Mountbattens (Louis, 1st Earl Mountbatten of Burma) and family, and they used to have royalty. We would always sit and watch and try to look out for the royalty going by', recalls Mrs Leggett.

Freda before her marriage.

'One day a gentleman stopped and asked my mother about the little girl in the bath chair. He said he would back a horse that day and that he would give my mother the winnings.' The man was as good as his word. Back he came, and he duly handed over the money. 'I have often wondered who that man was,' Mrs Leggett admits.

Sadly Dorothy didn't live long. She died in 1918 when Spanish flu swept the country. 'There were no antibiotics then.'

Mrs Leggett, who now lives in Chichester, was born in Arundel Road, Boxgrove. Her mother was one of 13 children, but Mrs Leggett was just one of two. Her father was a farm worker, and the family moved to Lavant when Mrs Leggett was five. She remembers well the school. Mr Young was the schoolmaster, and the children were very strictly brought up. As for entertainment, they made their own. 'We used to have hoops and skipping ropes and we used to play rounders. We didn't have swimming pools or things like that.' These were the days of candles and these were the days of a shared well for water. But there were other compensations. These were the days when no one ever needed to lock a door. 'We always felt very safe,' Mrs Leggett recalls.

And the family was close. Stories would be told around the fire, and a cylinder-type gramophone provided the music. As for washing, water would be heated in a big pot on the open grate. 'Mum would wash me

Freda's tragic sister Dorothy.

Left: *George and Freda Leggett on their wedding day.*

Freda and George Leggett with their daughter Dorothy Rose, April 1928.

and my sister and then when we had gone to bed, mum and dad would reheat the water and have their bath. That was the way of life.'

But sadness wasn't long in coming. Dorothy's death in 1918 was followed by the death of their mother just six years later. 'She was very unfortunate to die at the age of 47. It was called a tumour. If she had been here today, they would have called it cancer. But we always said that after my sister died, she more or less lost the will to live. My sister was the invalid, and mum had given her whole life to looking after her.'

Within a couple of years of losing her mother, though, Mrs Leggett found herself gaining a husband at Lavant Church on a warm day in 1926. 'You didn't invite people along in those days. People used to come along uninvited and they were always welcome.' The marriage was the culmination of a courtship much of which was spent in Chichester cinemas, particularly the Odeon (now Iceland in South Street). Mrs Leggett's husband was a soldier when she first met him, and she admits even now her weakness for a uniform. 'I just loved his uniform. He looked so smart!'

[7 May 1998]

Life at the House

Mountbatten and his young family are among Edith Knights' recollections of Adsdean House in Funtington. Mrs Knights says she finds it difficult to understand how the house, now flats, has disappeared from memory.

She remembers well A.H.Tennant, a millionaire who lived in Adsdean House when she was a girl in the 1910s. Mr Tennant was the man who then rented it out to the Mountbattens, a distinguished, glamorous couple with the world at their feet.

'Mr Tennant used to go down to West Ashling post office every day in a huge black trap with a huge beautiful black horse,' Mrs Knights recalls. 'We children used to curtsey to him. Whether we were told to or not, I don't know, but the groom at the back used to smile.

21

'Adsdean House is still there but it is all flats now, but it was a beautiful place and it's sad that few people remember it how it was.'

Edith Knights.

Mrs Knights' late husband Walter worked there as a nursery footman after leaving an office job in Portsmouth. His time at Adsdean House coincided with the Mountbattens who moved there with their young family. 'Mountbatten was there for quite a few years. He was going to and fro to Portsmouth for the Navy.'

One of the changes Mountbatten brought to Adsdean House was a golf course, and the house itself became a key place for socialites and houseguests. 'He employed a terrific lot of people in those days and then of course he went to Malta for two years. My husband left because there was nobody there apart from a few maids.'

Left: *Adsdean House, Funtington.*

Above: *Edith's husband Walter.*

Mrs Knights recalls: 'My husband liked the Mountbattens. They were very nice people. When he didn't have any of his Navy fellows from Portsmouth, he used to get the footman to go on the golf course with him. Whether my husband used to play or just caddy, I don't remember. It's an awful long time ago now.'

One memory, though, which remains clear in Mrs Knights' mind is of a Christmas party at Adsdean House. 'I went to this party for the servants there, and the Mountbattens came in with their guests, and I remember distinctly Princess Marina and Princess Ingrid of Sweden. I remember that there were lots of others, but they were so distinctive in their dresses.'

The Mountbattens were invariably kind to their servants, and there was never a shortage of good food to be had.

'But now it seem as though Adsdean House has been forgotten. It is as if it has just vanished. It is a terrific shame.'

[4 July 1996]

Thrashings and Fried Mice

Fried mice sandwiches and good thrashings are among the earliest memories of one of the grand old characters of East Dean.

Celebrated for his huge local knowledge and his profound sense of history, Arch Long readily evokes times and ways that have gone forever – some rather less lamented than others.

There was probably relief all round when one particular gipsy cure disappeared from the family armoury. As a young child, Arch suffered from bedwetting until, without his knowledge, the cure was tried on him – a fried mouse sandwich! He recalls: 'I couldn't understand why I was being offered food to eat when it wasn't meal time, but the cure worked and saved me from many thrashings!'

Arch's memories have been brought together in a new book, *Why Did They Call Me Archibald?*, compiled by Richard Pailthorpe and Janet Holt and published by the Weald and Downland Museum at Singleton.

Arch was born in the tiny West Sussex village of Heyshott in 1905, the 12th child in a family of 13, and his long memory instantly brings his childhood to life. From Heyshott, Arch's family moved to Upwaltham in 1908, and here his memories are of hardship and hunger. There were few items of furniture in the cottage, and the Long children were kept busy with household tasks, such as collecting kindling wood so that the range could be lit before their father left for work at 5a.m. Another task involved filling the copper for washing from the rainwater butt. Over the fire was kept a bushel-sized cauldron in which a stew of rabbit, turnip and split peas was kept simmering.

Breakfast consisted of porridge, bread, jam and tea, and hedgerow fruits would all be made into jam. But Arch remembers always being hungry as a child 'because there was just not enough food to go around a large family, although living in the country, one could always scrump an apple or eat a raw turnip'.

Chichester was a shopping destination, and Arch remembers his mother always taking the children around the Cathedral to look at the effigies. Market day in Chichester was on a Wednesday and all the approach roads would be full of sheep. 'There were so many thousands that it looked as though you were walking on their backs' he recalls.

As for entertainment, toys were scarce. A baby's first toy would be a pig's bladder filled with some peas to make a rattle. During the evening, tiddly-winks might be played or the girls might sing some of the popular songs of the day.

For Arch the move to East Dean, where he lives today, came in October 1915, and here it was inevitable that he should develop further his deep love and knowledge of the countryside. He would often go off on his own for long walks. Bird-nesting was a favourite hobby. Then came work, service in the army and the beginnings of a long association with Goodwood. But that's another story…

[17 March 1994]

Snapshots of Pre-War Life in Selsey

Jeanne and Arthur Slaughter were the daughter and son of two of the most important people in their respective communities.

Jeanne was the daughter of long-serving Selsey postman Richard Morey, and Arthur was the son of Birdham village policeman Jimmy Slaughter. Both men carried out their tasks in villages vastly different from the Selsey and Birdham of today.

Jeanne, now 82, remembers the heavy workload her father carried, back in pre-war Selsey. 'He did it all himself. He used to work Christmas

Day and Boxing Day. He would go into Chichester to get the post. They had a horse and cart. He used to start at about five in the morning and he would work all day. He started as a telegraph boy.'

Up in Birdham, Arthur's father policed by dint of the strength of his character and the sheer size of his hands.

Jeanne and Arthur met at the cinema in Selsey. Arthur still possesses some of the what's-on cards for the late 1930s, detailing the latest movies on show from the likes of Cary Grant and Flora Robson. 'My brother showed the films,' Jeanne recalls. 'It was always packed. It was sixpence to go in. They used to change the films about three times a week. People used to queue up, and that's where I met my husband.

'He used to come down on his motorbike. When we first met, I was 16 and he was 17, and we got talking outside the cinema. My sister met up with Arthur's mate, and that's how it began.'

They married in June 1940 and are looking forward to their 60th wedding anniversary this summer. They have lived in the same house in Seal Road, Selsey, for all their married life.

Arthur went into the Royal Engineers a couple of months before their wedding day; Jeanne – whose name is spelt the French way because of her father's First World War service in France – worked in Marks and Spencer's in Chichester and then in the World Stores.

Back in Selsey, she also did fire duty. 'We had to plot on the map where the bombs dropped and the places where the vehicles had to go. We had to answer the telephones and write it all down in the log book. I had to do that at about 11 at night and then at about six and then I used to catch the bus into Chichester to work.'

Selsey didn't escape the war unscathed, and its population greatly altered. There were plenty of Americans and Canadians around. Many of the houses were taken over. By some accounts, one or two of the local girls were also taken over. 'The Americans had the money, you see', Jeanne recalls. 'They certainly had more than the Brits.'

Since then, Selsey probably hasn't fared too well, the Slaughters reckon. Jeanne is nostalgic about her early days in the town – back when it was a village. 'Everybody knew each other. It was so friendly. It was

Left: *Arthur Slaughter after he set up a haulage business in the 1950s.*

Above: *Jeanne Slaughter in her fire service uniform during the war.*

Arthur, aged 14, on his bike in the lanes of Bracklesham Bay.

a nice little village, and now it has all changed. Where the houses are now it was all fields where we used to go blackberrying.'

[27 April 2000]

Meat is Fresh ... from the Garden Slaughterhouse

Some people have fairies at the bottom of their garden, but Madeline Thomas had a slaughterhouse.

Her father was Gilbert Ambrose, Westbourne's near-legendary butcher and a man still fondly remembered four years after his death. Born in 1906, Mr Ambrose left school at the age of 14 and entered the butcher's trade, gaining a good reputation far afield.

Mrs Thomas, who now lives in Northchapel, recalls: 'He used to go to market with his meat. Chichester was one market of course, but at one time he was going to four – Salisbury, Winchester and Fareham as well.

'We had a slaughterhouse down the bottom of our garden where he killed everything.

It was just something you lived with. It didn't seem strange.'

There wasn't much noise. 'Pigs would squeal as they were unloaded, but pigs would squeal if you so much as looked at them', Mrs Thomas recalls. 'They were killed as quickly as possible, of course. There wasn't any space to keep them, for a start.'

The slaughterhouse was in operation from five in the morning, four days a week, with seven or eight staff killing a weekly load of around 200 or 300 cattle and a couple of hundred pigs and lambs.

'I was born in 1943', Mrs Thomas says. 'After 1952, the slaughterhouse really got going. It was part and parcel of life. I am a farmer's wife now. That's how life is. You get to realise that meat isn't always neatly parcelled up.'

Mrs Thomas laments the passing of the small village butcher, a character forced out by changing ways and by supermarket dominance. Equally she laments the passing of a meat which simply tasted better and fresher, a meat free from additives and not impregnated with anything.

'I remember taking the meat round the village on a bike when I was small. It used to be busy during the week. That was the country way.'

But for all those who remember Mr Ambrose as a butcher, there will be just as many who remember him as a horseman. 'He just loved horses. His father was a coachman, and he was brought up on horses. In the 1910s there was no other way of getting around. He couldn't see a horse without wanting to touch it. It was in his blood.'

He started his driving with a little pony and trap; he graduated to shows and was soon touring the country with his horsebox. Villagers would always take an interest, asking him where he was off to as he hit the road for another show. His first horse was called 'Lady Westbourne', and thereafter he gave all his horses the Westbourne prefix, ensuring that the name of the village travelled the country wherever he went.

'He used to judge a lot. You could never keep him out of the ring. He was always in there, always involved. The cups he had were just incredible. His horses were always in physical perfection.'

[9 March 1995]

Photo brings back Flood of Memories

Memories of childhood eight decades ago came flooding back for a Chichester woman and her Nutbourne brother when they cast their eyes over a recent copy of the *Chichester Observer*.

Winifred Twine with her brother Leslie Gillingham.

Winifred Twine, now 89, and her 86-year-old brother Leslie Gillingham recognised themselves as tiny children in a family photograph dating back to about 1908. The picture showed them outside the Nutbourne post office which their parents John and Elizabeth, also pictured, ran until 1918. The Gillinghams started up a grocery – now Nutbourne stores – and added a bakery and then a post office.

Mrs Twine recalls: 'My father would sell everything, all the groceries, and there was nothing prepacked in those days. They had to cut the cheese and the lard and the bacon and weigh up the biscuits.'

Mr Gillingham, just a baby in a pram in the photo, remembers: 'With my sister we used to have the pony and cart around Chidham every Saturday delivering the bread and the cakes during the first war. There was an ammunition dump down in Chidham there. That's where a lot of people used to work. I suppose they were filling shells.'

Mrs Twine also remembers the pony and trap. It was an important way of getting into Chichester, though they often cycled. Then when she started school at the Central Girls, the train became the preferred means of transport – another way of getting into a city which Mrs Twine says has changed little since those days. 'It was very quiet though, then. Nutbourne was very quiet as well, even though it was on the main Brighton road.'

There was joy amid the tranquillity. 'We had some very happy days there. We used to play in the streets. There were no cars.'

Among the not quite so happy memories was the weekly Sunday ritual, which started with Sunday school at 10.15a.m., chapel at 11, then Sunday school again at 2.45p.m. before chapel once more at 6.30p.m.

'Sundays were Sundays then. You didn't play about in the streets. We had one little bike between us but we weren't allowed to use it. We had our best clothes on and that was it.'

As time passed, so new technologies came, and life began to change. Just before the Great War, the Gillinghams became the first family in the area to get a telephone. And that meant telegram duties for the children. Telegrams were phoned through to the post office, written down and then taken out by bike. Mrs Twine and Mr Gillingham well remember doing the deliveries and then waiting to see if there was a reply which needed to be phoned back.

Towards the end of the war, though, came the blow which was to end the Gillingham's days at the family store. News came through that their brother Wilfred, who would have taken over the business from his father, had been killed at Arras.

Mrs Twine recalls: 'I remember when the news came through. It was a telegram and it absolutely broke my father's heart. My mother was tougher, but my father was very soft-hearted.'

The family eventually moved to Chidham. Mr Gillingham senior and his wife both died in 1949, aged 78 and 82 respectively. But time hasn't dimmed the memories of those days in Nutbourne – days not much

short of a century ago. 'I don't think I'd fit into that pram now though!'
Mr Gillingham jokes.

[17 February 1994]

Secrets from Harry's Album

Maggie Wakeford reckons her relationship with her late father-in-law
was the kind of friendship you probably have only once in your life. A
countryman through and through, he was born in Priors Leaze Lane,
Hambrook, and lived there all his life. She still cherishes the photographs
he gave her in a slightly battered brown album. He never spoke about
the photographs, so she doesn't know how the slightly odd assortment
came together – images of mid-19th-century Chichester alongside scenes
of Goodwood and scenes of (presumably) rural Hambrook.

But while he didn't speak about the photographs, he did speak about
virtually all other aspects of his country life. In the last years before his
death nearly two years ago at the age of 85, Harry Wakeford was blind.
But with his country ways, in a sense he could still see.

'We would walk for miles and he would always know where everything
was,' Maggie says. 'He lived in Hambrook all his life. He had a market
gardening business. I didn't really get to know him until he lost his sight
and he needed help. He was very independent, as was his wife.

'He went blind seven or eight years ago, and having to depend on
somebody else was a very big step for him. But the friendship we had
was very special. It was very personal and very emotional at times.

'When his wife died, we never left him on his own. We sat on the
edge of the bed, sometimes for up to half an hour holding hands, with
not a word spoken.

'It was just a special bond. I don't think I ever felt that close to
anybody. I had my own mum and dad, and I loved them dearly, but this
was something special.'

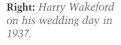

Right: *Harry Wakeford
on his wedding day in
1937.*

Below: *Harry is ready
for duty at the outbreak
of the Second World
War.*

Maggie recalls Harry as a countryman at heart, steeped in local lore. He remembered the village fete from its earliest days, long before it died and was resurrected.

'And he was as honest as the day was long. Everything had to be just right. He was in market gardening as was his father before him until they sold up in 1969. Even when he had lost his sight, he could still tell you exactly where everything was. I admired the man a lot. I just felt it was sad not having really known him before.'

In his lifetime he had the distinction of being one of only three people to have been born in Hambrook and to be living there still. Maggie believes the distinction now falls to just one person.

'He was a very quiet man. He was very private. He was very tidy, even in his blindness. If he washed his hands once, he would wash them a hundred times a day. He used to have a little stall outside his bungalow selling flowers. Everything was very regimented with him. He was so tidy. We used to think he was a fussy old devil, but he wasn't.'

Maggie says she keeps her memories of Harry tightly locked away. 'I am sure that the times I had with him are times that nobody else had. The fact that he was independent all his life meant that I don't think other people had that closeness with him.'

But he was also a man who was totally devoted to his wife. She came 'first, second and third' for everything. 'When she died, it was only six weeks later that he passed on. It was almost as if he had stayed alive to look after her and make sure she was OK.'

[26 April 2001]

One of the photographs from Harry's album shows Inlands Farm at Nutbourne in 1911. The farm was owned by the Wakeford brothers, Harry (Harry's father) and George.

Chapter Three

THE SECOND WORLD WAR COMES TO CHICHESTER

Bomb wiped out Three Generations

Margaret Mitchell left her home in Chapel Street, Chichester, for her weekly wartime treat – a Wednesday afternoon trip to the pictures. When she got home, her house was a pile of rubble. Five members of her family – including her 18-month-old daughter – were dead. Baby Brenda's shoes and part of her pram were found in Priory Park 500 yards away. For one family, the war had hit home – their home – in the most horrific way imaginable.

It's impossible to believe that anyone could get over a tragedy of such dimensions. Looking back, Margaret's husband Alfred reckons she never did. She lived on for many years, but was never the same person.

As for Mr Mitchell, now 82 and still living in Chichester, it was six weeks or so before the news reached him. 'I was just outside Algiers, serving in the First Army. You've heard of the Eighth Army? Well, the First Army landed on the other side of Rommel and opened up a second front. That was why he lost. Yet you never hear of the First Army, even though they were the most important thing there was. Anyway, it must have been about six weeks after the bomb hit my house that I was called in by the commanding officer who broke the news.'

A tragic family … Alfred Mitchell's aunt Hilda on the day she married Alf Tester. Hilda was killed with her five-year-old daughter Vera when a bomb dropped on the Mitchell home. Also killed were Alfred Mitchell's grandfather George (pictured here wearing a trilby hat, second from right at the back) and his mother Ethel.

At a stroke, Mr Mitchell had lost three generations of his family. His mother Margaret was dead; so too were his daughter and his grandfather George. Also killed were his aunt, Hilda Tester and her five-year-old daughter Vera. 'The officer just called me into the office and told me. It was a shock, but you don't really react in those circumstances. They did try to help me as much as they could. They let me lie in a bit and everybody was very good.

'But I certainly couldn't go home. I tried, but there was a war on. I couldn't get home at all. There was no hope of that. The reason I couldn't was because my wife was not injured. She was saved because she had gone to the pictures.

'It was a Wednesday afternoon at about 4p.m. when it happened. The bomb hit my home at 24 Chapel Street. There was an empty house next door, and that went as well.

'My wife used to go to the pictures every Wednesday. She left my grandfather to look after the child while she had a couple of hours' peace and relaxation.

'My aunt Mabel had a little girl, and she used to go around there with them, but that particular day she decided not to go because she was a bit late. Because of that she lived. Her daughter still calls on me now.'

The bomb dropped in 1943. Mr Mitchell had gone out to Africa the year before, and he was there for 18 months in all. 'I copped this skin disease and was in hospital for six months. They couldn't clear it up and eventually they sent me home on a troop ship. I was in Southport for a while. When I came back to England I was put in hospital. They let me out and I went into a billet. I stayed there for perhaps two or three weeks, and then I was told I could go home awaiting recall. I went home and was there for perhaps three weeks.'

Alfred and Margaret Mitchell on their wedding day in Chichester, 1940.

His wife, understandably, was not a well woman. 'She was not very well at all, and she never was after that. She got Parkinson's disease, and they think it was the shock that brought it on. She died six years ago, but she never got over what happened. She was never the same woman.'

As for Mr Mitchell, he coped – simply because he had to. 'After 18 months or whatever, you start to get over it. There was a war on, and you have to think of other things. Unless you have been in a war, you won't understand. I can't explain what it's like, but in a way it helped.'

Mr and Mrs Mitchell had a daughter a couple of years after the war ended, and Mr Mitchell is now a grandfather twice over and a great-grandfather three times.

But he admits it would have been nice to have a second daughter to look after him. Not that he's complaining: 'I have never been ill in all my life. I don't suffer much at all these days,' he says.

[26 August 1999]

The Day the Bombs fell

Cyril Perrott, aged 20.

Former Chichester schoolmaster Cyril Perrott remembers vividly the moment he saw the bomb doors open to loose their deadly load on the city. Mr Perrott, a woodwork teacher at the Lancastrian Boys School for 30 years until his retirement in 1964, was cycling by the Cathedral on the day Chichester suffered its worst bomb damage of the war.

He recalls: 'It would have been about 1942. The Germans had the idea of sending planes towards our coast, mostly putting down bombs in the Southampton area and then running along the coast, Chichester, Bognor Regis, Eastbourne, dropping bombs as they went.

'On this particular afternoon I had left school and I was cycling home to Fishbourne and I had done a bit of shopping and had a basket on the front of the bike.

'It was raining, not very heavily, and there were very few people about. Just as I was between A&N and the Cathedral, I saw this German plane coming along from the west, flying not much more than 200 foot over County Hall.

'To my astonishment I saw the bomb doors open, and I think it was three bombs came out. As I was in the Home Guard, I had been trained to get down flat when bombs came down. I got down in the gutter and some of my shopping was floating in the rainwater.'

Shop windows were shattered by the blast and a number of people were killed.

Mr Perrott recalls particularly the bomb which landed in North Street. Because it wasn't dropped from any great height, it didn't hit the ground end on. As a result, it bounced and went through the wall of a big haberdasher's on the eastern side of the street. Women working there watched, unharmed, as the bomb came through the near wall, penetrated the far wall and exploded in St Martin's Street where it wrecked two houses and killed several people.

The dent in North Street where it first landed was visible outside Woolworth's for many years. The site of the destroyed houses – Chichester's last bomb site – has just been sold for redevelopment.

Staff at the Lancastrian Boys School in about 1936. Mr Perrott is second from the right in the front row. Headmaster Mr Trotter is in the middle of the front row.

But such destruction was far from being an everyday occurrence for wartime Cicestrians, says Mr Perrott, whose daily experience of the war was more along the lines of tramping down to the dug-out with his pupils. Now 89, he recalls the countless times school had to be abandoned because of an air-raid warning. The pupils were never afraid, cheerfully accepting the disruption. Teachers would try to continue lessons where possible, otherwise the option was verbal games.

Mr Perrott, who arrived in Chichester in 1934, also remembers the 1940s as a time when the city had three cinemas all full to bursting. 'They were all absolutely full all the afternoon and all the evening because the troops were coming in from all about.'

Looking back on his six decades in the city, Mr Perrott says Chichester has changed dramatically. It now boasts many more people and much more traffic. Sixty years ago as he stepped from the station, he saw a medieval farm house and a row of medieval cottages. Now the site boasts the bus station and the law courts.

But overall, Chichester has retained its cathedral city charm, Mr Perrott says.

'The people in charge of Chichester who dominate its development have made a fair job. They have saved the cathedral city atmosphere.'

[24 March 1994]

'Boy' – Victim of the Petworth Bombing

Ron Thatcher can't even remember his cousin's proper name. Everyone knew him simply as 'Boy'. The poor lad didn't have the chance to become anything else. His wasn't a long life. In September 1942, 'Boy' became one of the 29 victims of the German bombs which wrecked Petworth Boys School.

Mr Thatcher, a life-long Fittleworth resident, was working for a firm called Petworth Engineering Company at the time. 'I was about 16 years old then. We dealt with country house lighting plants. A lot of places in those days didn't have electricity. We were going down to the railway at Petworth that day.

'As we were driving along Pound Street, roughly half way, I heard this airplane engine very loud. Coming towards us was a Junkers 88. There was just one.

'It was a very grey, damp, almost drizzly morning. The cloud was very low. It was one of those really nasty mornings. When I heard the engine, it was so low that the markings on the plane were clearly visible.

'And then I looked and saw the bombs come out, one by one. It was so close. It was flying parallel to Pound Street, very slightly to the west side.'

Some people say four bombs dropped. That's perfectly possible, though Mr Thatcher remembers only three. What he remembers most is the fact that they didn't dip. They remained perfectly horizontal as they fell to the ground.

'I remember the noise of the impact.'

Mr Thatcher carried on with his business. He didn't go to the scene then, and he didn't go later. 'We had a job to do. We just went on. I know that when we got down to the railway, the landlord, just by there, came

Growing up with war ... a young Ron Thatcher.

'Boy' – a tragic victim of the Second World War. He is pictured on the left. On the right is his sister Anne. Joyce Balchin is in the foreground. The identity of the boy in the middle is not known.

out and said "I am awfully sorry to tell you that those bombs you saw hit the boys school."'

Along with the boys, the headmaster and a teacher died. Among the pupils was 'Boy', Mr Thatcher's cousin and son of 'Morry' Balchin. 'He would have been about nine or ten. I really can't be sure. But he was a lovely little chap, rather round-faced.'

Whether the school was actually targeted has been a matter of debate ever since. From the way the plane was heading, Mr Thatcher is inclined to think the school bombing was simply bad luck. 'It is known fact that the bombs ricocheted. For some reason, they didn't explode on impact. They must have gone up and come down again.' Again he stresses it's conjecture, but Mr Thatcher reckons a much more likely target would have been the complex at the back of Leconfield House.

Mr Thatcher speaks with a lifetime's experience of the area. An only child, he was born in Fittleworth in 1927. His family took him at the age of six weeks to a house just a hundred or so yards from the house, opposite the village hall, in which he now lives.

When Mr Thatcher was born, his father was probably driving for Sayers of Fittleworth. 'They did the school coaches, and they had the lorries. I think my father was doing lorry driving down there. Mum was just a housewife.'

Mr Thatcher went to the old Fittleworth School. 'I started off as an infant there. The infants class was a hutted classroom. It was a good school. I think the teachers made it good. They were excellent teachers. I don't think I ever caused anyone much trouble as far as I can recall. We all have our little skirmishes, but the discipline was pretty strong. We never seemed to get into any real trouble though.'

He remembers the headmaster Mr Bowyer and his wife with particular affection: 'He was a strict headmaster, but he and his wife were very kind. Because my mum had rheumatoid arthritis, there was one time I went to stay with them for a few days. They looked after me in the school house.

'Soon after I was born, my mother got rheumatoid arthritis which got progressively worse until just before the war broke out when she had a more or less total collapse due to the pain and immobility.

'As the war broke out, her doctor got called up, and I think that the big trouble then was that she was allowed to lie in bed. In those days they allowed you to do it. My dad had to work, so she was allowed to lie in bed and went through the war years in bed. It probably wasn't the right thing to do.'

[14 October 1999]

Cathedral suffered a Near Miss

A close shave for Chichester Cathedral is one of the wartime memories of a city man who served throughout the war as a part-time fireman. Stanley Wells, aged 83, remembers particularly the day catastrophe nearly hit the streets of Chichester. It was the day he watched a doodlebug whizz past perilously close to the Cathedral.

Mr Wells, who lives in Chichester, joined the Auxiliary Fire Service – AFS – just before the war, and the result was years of action in the thick of bomb damage and near disaster. 'Things always seemed to hot up around 4a.m. when the Germans were dropping a few over Tangmere,' says Mr Wells. And he also recalls two bombs going down by the police station.

But one of the memories which burns brightest is the day he saw Chichester Cathedral just yards from destruction. 'I remember seeing four doodlebugs in all. They used to come along with sparks coming out the back. I lived in Franklin Place at the time. I was getting up at that time at about 6a.m.

'You could see the Cathedral from the back bedrooms, and a doodlebug went by the Cathedral tower, lower than the steeple. It landed somewhere up Compton way. I actually saw the thing go by. If they had hit the Cathedral, there would have been quite a bit of damage', Mr Wells recalls.

But more often, any activity overhead was directed elsewhere, either further north or Portsmouth. 'We used to be on duty and you could hear them groaning overhead as the bombers were going on to Liverpool, Coventry or wherever. You couldn't see them, but you could hear them, though you could see the searchlights going.' Overall there was not much damage in Chichester, but the glow of bomb-ravaged Portsmouth was often visible in West Sussex. 'The sky was lit up. It was mostly incendiaries.'

Closer to home, Mr Wells also had a rather too close encounter with a German machine-gunner while he was working at the Charlton sawmills.

And even on his way home from work, the war was never far away. Coming back through Goodwood one day, he witnessed a dogfight between an enemy and a Tangmere fighter. 'This German pilot was shot down or baled out, and he was in a tree up at Shopwhyke. I saw the body up the tree, but we couldn't do anything about it.'

In all, Mr Wells spent 46 years working in sawmills including Slindon and then back to Charlton, but his AFS days finished just after the war, marking the close of a fiery nine years.

[27 January 1994]

Chichester celebrates the end of the war in Europe on VE Day, 8 May 1945.

Those Nights with no Light

John and Muriel Hill well remember the busy life their father led as one of Chichester's air-raid wardens. Harold Hill, a cabinet maker by profession, joined the wardens in 1941 and was soon kitted out in the characteristic tunic.

Muriel recalls: 'When the siren went he had to get out all his gear, get on his tunic, the gaiters and boots, and off he would go.'

She remembers how frightening that siren could be in the early days. John is living proof that you had to think quickly. 'This Jerry came out of the sky and was going to machine-gun us so they put me down behind the wall,' said John.

Chichester didn't suffer anything like the bomb damage suffered by Portsmouth or Southampton, but the damage was still significant.

John and Muriel, who still live in Chichester, recall damage to both Little London and Armadale Road, the latter when the Germans were aiming for the plotting station at St James' School. They also recall the Liberator bomber which came down on Chichester laundry, one of the worst moments the city endured. 'I had an aunt, and we were sitting having a cup of tea, and the blast knocked the cups off the table. Some of the ceiling came down too,' John said. 'I think one of the laundry girls went back to the laundry to get her pay packet and got killed.'

Muriel, who was a young girl at the time, remembers: 'Somebody else had a narrow escape with one of the wheels which came off the plane. I think it landed on one of the roofs.'

Their father, who died in 1980 aged 78, remained a warden throughout the war, putting in countless hours whenever duty demanded. 'I suppose he was at risk. He must have been. He was never hurt, though', Muriel said.

'When he went out to a site he would have to fill out a form, putting all the details, saying where it happened, all about the casualties, what roads

*Chichester marks
United Nations Day,
14 June 1942.*

were blocked.' The report would also require details of any unexploded
bombs, plus details of any services already on the spot or hurrying to
the scene. While dad was out doing this, the chances are that John and
Muriel were in the safety of the dug-out – a vivid memory still for John
as he looks back on his wartime boyhood.

For Muriel, the big memory is of the austerity which was their daily
experience. 'People had to queue up for food. We didn't have eggs. We
had ration books and had little coupons which we had to use. I don't
know what it was called, but there was always a big queue for the cake
shop in St Pancras.'

Then after the hustle and bustle of the day came the pitch dark of
night when no light was tolerated: 'The wardens would be out checking
up. Everybody had to have black-out curtains up, and you were in trouble
if you didn't.'

[7 July 1994]

Stuka Terror hits Sussex

Fifty-four years ago today Thorney Island, Ford and other airfields near
Chichester were attacked in a massive air raid. Within seconds of each
other, four of the Stukas were brought down by fighters over the Bosham
area. One plane came down at the Broyle, diving vertically into a field
near the school and coming to grief in what is now a housing estate.
A second plane dived into the mud at Dell Quay, both crew escaping;
a third crashed to the north-west near the railway line; and the fourth
crashed in a field at Chidham.

Just two days before, on 16 August 1940, Tangmere was attacked by
29 Stukas whilst a further 50 raided targets at Portsmouth and on the
Isle of Wight. Nine were shot down, three crashing on dry land near
Chichester. One crash-landed through a hedge on farmland at South
Mundham with dead or dying crew. It remained on site, was stripped of
souvenirs and was visited by half the population of Bognor Regis.

A second aircraft crashed across the B2145 road near Selsey, and the third dived smoking into a meadow near Pagham Harbour, killing the crew.

Between them, the two raids just two days apart live on vividly in the minds of many residents of Chichester and Bognor. For Ian Hutton, who lives at Liphook, they have become a source of endless fascination.

He has researched the raids and their implications and now possesses a wealth of information, including first-hand accounts.

'It all started when I was walking on the South Downs Way and saw this memorial stone near West Dean. I thought "whatever has happened here?", and I started to ask around.

'I have managed to track down some witnesses to some of the action and have been researching it for about three years. What I have really focused on are the August 1940 battles. The point about these Stukas is that they are famous aircraft and nearly everyone remembers them.

'A lot of people I am talking to are confirming what others are saying, and a picture is emerging. It's a piece of local history, something which went deep into the minds of people around here.'

The South Mundham Stuka was shot down after bombing Tangmere airfield and while making its escape southwards. It crashed between trees along a hedgerow, tearing off the ends of its wings before landing in the only unobstructed field in the area. All the others had counter-invasion measures installed. The plane rolled to a halt with the engine still racing. Gun crews raced towards it. They found the pilot dead and the gunner severely wounded.

British artillerymen had difficulty in switching off the engine, fumbling with the switches on the instrument panel. Once the engine was stilled and peace returned to the countryside, the pilot's body was rolled into a blanket and placed in a ditch.The Stuka remained there for several days, left to the attention of local people who gradually stripped off all the parts that could be removed. Some say that the pilot was left in the ditch for two days before being removed for burial.

On the 30th anniversary of the raid on Thorney Island, former Stuka pilot Otton Schmidt recalled his part in the operation.

Writing in the early 1970s, he recalled 18 August as a beautiful summer's day. His instructions were simple: attack targets on the English mainland.

'It was all so calm and peaceful', he wrote. 'The coast suddenly popped up in front of us. We could make out Thorney Island, and we intended to go down one after another on the target.

'The leading aircraft looked like a string of pearls as they started to go in. Then by chance I looked out and from out of the sun came the first wedge of British fighters, all screaming towards us!

'Initial evasive action brought my own flight to safety, but the British fighters' speed left me speechless, and we didn't expect the last flight in our formation to take the brunt of their attack.

'One Junkers 87 went into the sea like a flaming torch, I remember, and all this time there were no sounds or words on our radio. There was no time to think about what was happening. The main thing was to remember the correct moment to start the attack.

'And now it was my turn. First I made the wing waddle, indicating I was about to dive, then applied the dive brakes. Next I shut the radiators, adjusted my bomb sight and pointed the nose on target.

'Now my vision was only downwards! What had happened up to now was nothing. By this time, I saw the two arms of Thorney Island which gave me a fix on the airfield. I could see six aircraft hangars close to one another and not far from them some shelters. Certainly, below me, were several of the 24 multi-engined machines we had pinpointed on our recce photographs.

'The hangar complex grew within my sights, and without any correction I dropped lower and lower. Then, at last, there was just one hangar trapped in my sight cross wires.

'I pressed my bomb-button – and my job was done. All I had to do now was to get the aircraft on an even keel and make for home.'

[18 August 1994]

City's Wartime 'Mum in a Million'

The anguish of a mother whose son is away fighting is something most people can barely imagine. But Chichester woman Annie Wyatt endured the agonies seven times over during the Second World War. She had seven sons. All seven went to war and all seven returned safe and sound: William, John, Tom, Frank, Gordon, Ron and Roger fought for their country and survived.

Only Roger is still alive and lives in Vancouver. Of the men's four sisters, only Dorothy Watkins survives, and she lives in Chichester.

Her mother's great contribution was something which won her a special place in the hearts of Cicestrians, Mrs Watkins recalls. Just a few weeks after the VE Day celebrations of May 1945, 73-year-old Annie Wyatt became Chichester's Battle Of Britain Mother. Mrs Watkins still keeps the press cutting of her mother's great day. Carnival queen competitions in Chichester had become old hat, so the local Royal Air Force Association decided to come up with something different.

Mrs Wyatt had lived in Chichester for the past 29 years. Her contribution to the war made her the ideal person to celebrate. Her attendants were a war widow of the First World War and a woman whose husband was an airman stationed at Tangmere during the Battle of Britain.

Dorothy Watkins moves into Chichester's first post-war prefab, in Swanfield Drive.

Entry qualifications for the competition were that entrants had to be over 35, mothers, and must have had either a husband or a child serving in the forces during the Battle of Britain. The three successful contestants were chosen from 12 who mounted the platform at the Grand Cinema.

Annie and Jack Wyatt.

Mrs Watkins recalls: 'I was about 24 or 25 at the time. We were all encouraging her to take part. I think she won by the amount of applause that the family gave her!

'It was just after VE Day. It was fine weather. It must have been about June, I should think. They had a procession through the town. She went through the streets and was very proud. It was really quite something.'

Mrs Wyatt proved a popular choice for the title, roundly backed by the audience and by the official judges, Dr S. Lewis, Mr G.E. Pullet and Mr E.A.K. Knight.

In the first precious days of peace Chichester celebrated all those who had done their bit. In Mrs Wyatt, the city had found a mother in a million.

[4 May 1995]

Crash fuels Old Memories

One of Chichester's worst moments of the war could so easily have brought devastation on a colossal scale. The Liberator which hit the city in May 1944 came within feet of crashing onto thousands of gallons of fuel. Four people were killed, 27 injured and a staggering 704 houses were damaged.

But wartime tanker driver Charles Slingo knows that the tragedy could so easily have been much much worse. The death toll could easily have run into hundreds. It is a moment Mr Slingo recalls vividly. He was standing in the depot. Nearby, four or five lorries were lined up, all filled with fuel. Then over came the stricken plane, just feet away. 'It came over just above our heads. I thought that was it. I thought we were going to be killed', Mr Slingo says. 'Then suddenly we heard the crash. It crashed in Kenneth Long's wood yard and set fire to the electric laundry.'

Mr Slingo, aged 79, of Oliver Whitby Road, recalls: 'We'd thought that that was our lot. We had quite a few tankers outside the depot. We wouldn't have had a chance to run.

'If it had come down on the fuel, then the whole street would have gone up, I imagine. The destruction would have been huge.'

The Liberator crash was far from being Mr Slingo's only close shave of the war.

His duties as a tanker driver were to supply the nearby aerodromes, servicing Tangmere, Ford and Thorney Island, plus the satellites at Apuldram, Selsey, Merston, Lagness, Funtington and Westhampnett. He worked 12-hour shifts, often at night when black-out restrictions limited his head-lamps to just a slit. Inevitably, driving around the narrow country lanes in pitch darkness with a massive load of fuel brought plenty of frightening moments.'It was murder driving at times, especially when it was foggy. I really don't know how I managed it.'

At times he would have to go to the Shell depot at Hamble, and on one occasion he came back past Portsmouth at the height of a bombing raid. 'I had 1,500 gallons of fuel. It was pretty scary. You heard bombs dropping all around you and just hoped for the best.'

Other duties would take him on a night-time tour of farms, supplying them with vaporising oil for their tractors. 'It was usually at night, and

Charles Slingo, pictured in the 1960s.

all you had was a torch as you went round. Sometimes I would be up the hills Chilgrove way, and in the dark and in the fog, it could get pretty worrying. I got lost a good two or three times!'

[25 May 1995]

Saved by Trees as Bomber crashed

The events of a spring day more than 50 years ago are vividly clear in the mind of Mary Evans. It was the day a Liberator bomber crashed on Chichester.

The news this week [25 April 1996] that proposed redevelopment work on the site will mean an alert over the possibility of unexploded bombs has brought the memories back all the more strongly.

Miss Evans, who returned to the city last year after many years away, was just 14 at the time and living at The Peacheries at the end of Bognor Road. 'I remember one evening we were out in the garden in a little tiny wood and it was so hot that we were under the trees which was a good job because one of our planes had a bomb on board and it was flying very low and it exploded right over the top of us.

'Parts of the plane rained down on the open space of the garden; parts were caught up in the trees. The laundry, which was next door to the school, was hit by the plane itself ... We lay down flat burying our heads by putting our hands across the back of our necks as we had been taught. When it was over we all ran towards the school straight through the French window.'

There was glass everywhere and the grass was on fire, Miss Evans recalls.

'We were rushed into the cellar until everything became quiet when we were brought out and sent home. They also brought in the wounded from the laundry next door and gave them first aid which they did to any of us that needed it.

'I was untouched and sent to walk home with a girl who lived in Bognor. Her parents later came and fetched her from my house. The whole experience was terrifying.'

Miss Evans recalls that the war brought many disturbed nights. 'The fighters came to attack London and on their return they dropped bombs so as to empty them out before they crossed the channel. There were sirens and searchlights going all night and much of the time was spent downstairs.' There was an Anderson shelter under the table, though the family also squashed together in the cupboard under the stairs. 'It was all very cosy in there as we had a chair and some blankets and would often snuggle up and tell stories, but it did mean that we had very little sleep which didn't help our health or education progress as we were constantly tired.

Some of the damage caused by the Liberator crash on Chichester.

40

Above: *Lionel Evans, a special constable during the Second World War.*

Right: *Lionel Evans and a Danish trainee picking peaches for Covent Garden market.*

'Occasionally school was cancelled, particularly at the beginning as the evacuees had to use our school so we often had lessons in the mornings or afternoons only and were given work to do for the rest of the time which, of course, we did reluctantly.'

At this time, Miss Evans' sister went to help their mother at the canteens which were set up all over the city to give servicemen coffee, tea and food. Their father became a special constable. It was a time when everyone was doing something for the war effort.

'As a girl guide I was expected to take part in the war effort which, for me, mostly consisted of sitting in the sewing-room at the local hospital embroidering the logo on to the corners of the sheets.

'It seemed a terrible waste of time to me, but it was probably the only way of getting it done. I also tried knitting socks and scarves for the soldiers but my efforts always resulted in large holes and misshapen garments.'

Miss Evans' favourite contribution towards the war effort was being a casualty for the first-aiders. 'They would practise making slings, put splints on legs and generally bandage me up which was tremendous fun.'

[25 April 1996]

'Teddy' Remembers

The *Chichester Observer* can count an illustrious name among its readers. A Prime Minister, no less. Sir Edward Heath contacted the *Observer* after reading a 'Remember When' feature several weeks ago on wartime Fishbourne. It prompted fond memories for the former premier. He was particularly amused to learn that his time near Chichester had been captured in verse. The poem, written by Esme Smuts who is now living in South Africa, evoked artillery officers at the *Woolpack Inn*:

An inn down Fishbourne way,
Into which the Major oft did stray.

The poem continues:

The Major often had a few,
And Teddy and Harry and Gibby too.

Teddy is now Sir Edward. At the time he was just a few years away from becoming a Member of Parliament and a little matter of 28 years away from becoming Prime Minister. Sir Edward, who ended the war as a major, says he remembers Esme Smuts well and that he was delighted to read her poem in the *Observer*, but he admits he had no idea she had written it. 'I was very interested to see the article in the paper. She obviously enjoyed writing the verse!'

Mrs Smuts was a subaltern in charge of the Ack-Ack at Fishbourne Cottage by the railway station. Mention of the cottage in the *Observer* brought a swift request for more information from Sir Edward.

Former Prime Minister Edward Heath returns to Chichester in 1998 to promote a book, and is shown being greeted by bookshop manager Shelagh Fraser. It was a trip which brought back memories of his wartime service in Fishbourne.

The cottage has been incorporated into maisonettes and is now part of Dolphin Court, but 50 years later Sir Edward remembers it well.

Mrs Smuts was attached to 107 HAA Regt RA, and Sir Edward was its adjutant. In all, Teddy Heath spent three or four months in the Chichester area before going north to Northumberland. Much of the time was spent in preparation for the move, and the regiment was on duty the whole time – all of which meant there was little time for getting to know Chichester: 'We all worked very hard', he says.

But Sir Edward recalls that even in those busy days the city reserved a warm welcome: 'We were received very well by the people of Chichester. It was a good base.' Particularly agreeable was being able to go to a restaurant from time to time, he recalls.

But as for any little anecdotes from the time, Sir Edward says the one which most readily springs to mind relates to the unprintable capers of someone else … a story best kept private.

[6 October 1994]

Chapter Four

THE CHILDREN OF THE SECOND WORLD WAR

The Dogfight Dangers

Neil Theobald remembers not quite knowing what war was when it broke out in 1939.

He was just four and a half at the time, and he remembers trying to fathom the enormity of it all with a five-year-old chum. But it wasn't long before the war was starting to impact on his every-day life.

Gas mask lessons became all part of a day's schooling for Neil and his friends down at the Witterings. School had been moved to the East Wittering parish hall, a building sadly no longer there.

'One of the lessons that we had to do was to take evasive action against a gas attack,' Mr Theobald recalls. 'I remember at a given signal we all had to fall to the ground, wherever we were, with our hands under our faces to give us a breathing space. I don't know if this would have worked!

'This was before we received our gas masks. When we did receive our gas masks, they were issued to us in a cardboard box, with a piece of string attached. My mother, I remember, made a cloth cover for the cardboard box to fit into, and a strap to fit over our shoulders.'

The war was coming closer.

Mr Theobald, now 59, of Stocks Lane, East Wittering, saw a slice of the action when he sneaked a look at the D-Day invasion rehearsals at Bracklesham. He remembers, too, the day headteacher Mrs Baker kept the pupils in because a dogfight was raging overhead. 'When we didn't arrive home at the correct time, our mothers came to find us and take us home. We would much rather have watched the dogfight than be dragged indoors!'

After 18 months' schooling at the parish hall, Mr Theobald moved up to the school at West Wittering. 'One day my sister Myra and I were blackberrying in a meadow to the side of our back garden when yet another dogfight was taking place. We were happily watching the action when our mother called to us to come in. As we were running down the path of our back garden, a spent cannon shell case fell from the sky and just missed my sister's head.' Not surprisingly, the shell case is still in the Theobald family to this day.

It was around this time that the pre-D-Day troop build-up began, with gun emplacements beginning to appear along the seafront. An emplacement of heavy guns was deployed at Cakeham Tower, and when these guns were firing, everything in the house would shake. 'Tank traps were built on the sands of the beach, built of metal poles similar to the scaffolding that is used in the building industry today. And along the cliff

tops behind the gun emplacements, huge concrete blocks were built.' For children, the blocks were close enough together for them to be able to run along the tops, jumping over the gaps.

'Later on in the war the guns' crews became quite good at firing at the flying bombs and turning them back to sea.

'Also at Cakeham a metal radar tower was built. I am not sure of the true function, but I remember that it gave us a lot of amusement trying to climb it. Looking back it was a silly thing to do!'

But it wasn't all fun and games. The nights Portsmouth was bombed were frightening, even from the Witterings. 'Mother would set all our clothes out on our beds, ready for a quick dash if things got really bad. Fortunately it didn't happen.

'I can remember mother and a few of the neighbours standing in our hallway listening to the guns and bombs falling on Portsmouth, hoping they were in the safest place.'

Around about this time the Canadian Black Watch began to arrive in the village, warriors warmly welcomed by many as part of the family. One of them ended up marrying Mr Theobald's eldest sister. 'We didn't know at that time that these men were being made ready for the fateful raid on Dieppe. When this happened, the village was devastated because of the amount of our friends that were killed ... My brother-in-law Carl was wounded, but survived and returned to England.'

Then came the Americans, white and coloured, but not billeted to-gether – a sad sign of the times. But the racial tensions weren't something to worry the West Sussex children. They had their eyes on other things. The Americans came bearing gifts. 'One thing that is remembered about the Yanks, us being kids, was the gum and candies that they gave us.'

[5 May 1994]

Left: *Neil Theobald's class at West Wittering Parochial School, c.1946. Neil is third from the right in the second row from the back. His sister Myra is fifth from the left in the second row from the front.*

Above: *A young Neil Theobald.*

Memories of a Wartime Education

Does anyone remember the sad fate of the soup which Mary Evans made for her cookery exam? Her friend Maureen mistakenly thought it was the washing-up water.

And what about Pat Seaman, the girl acrobat from Bognor who performed to a professional standard and was the envy of everyone? Did fame come her way?

It might all be more than half a century ago, but Jane Pearce still remembers fondly and in detail her Chichester schooldays.

Jane – then Farley and then going under her first name Audrey – was at Chichester High School for Girls from 1940-46. It was a wartime education in Stockbridge Road enlivened during the Blitz by frequent dashes to air-raid shelters.

Jane says it's impossible to imagine how the girls back then would have viewed the fact that the site is now lined up as part of a multi-million pound leisure centre.

She reckons a healthy chortle-cum-giggle would be the most likely reaction, particularly at the thought of a six-screen cinema. After all, their favourite weekend jaunt was to the Odeon, the Gaumont or the Exchange.

They would be there most Saturdays – and on Sundays as well if they had enough pocket money left. Jane recalls that they would choose the 1s 9d seats to watch the latest Gregory Peck, Alan Ladd or Gary Cooper films.

Jane also recalls the difficulties of the day. 'Accommodation was cramped when Streatham High School was evacuated to merge with Chi High during the Blitz. Upper-fifth class was housed in one of the laboratories, with shelving outside the room replacing their desks. The girls discovered that Miss Millard had a habit of popping into the store room for a quiet ciggy when smoke wafted through the slightly-open door from time to time.'

Temporary classrooms were erected in the grounds early in the 1940s, and air-raid shelters were dug around the edge of the playing fields. If the all-clear siren hadn't sounded by the time it was time to go home, the girls needed written permission from their parents to leave the shelter to catch their bus or train. 'Some teachers tried in vain to continue teaching when the siren went and all forms trooped to their respective shelters, but it never worked. Minimal lighting and the excitement of leaving school work behind ensured plenty of chatter and movement.'

Jane recalls that school entertainments included ballroom dancing classes which began at lunch time for the sixth form. Two girls from the upper-fifth were asked to provide strict tempo piano accompaniment to the quickstep, waltz and tango.

'Many girls who went to Miss Lombard's ballet school just naturally glided into her Saturday morning dancing lessons. Monthly dances at the school provoked many wails of "I've got nothing to wear" as clothing coupons rationed one's wardrobe.'

Another entertainment was the dogfights. Without any apparent thought for their own safety, many girls watched dogfights over Tangmere between German and British planes. 'When a plane crashed near Funtington, those living nearby did not consider themselves ghoulish for picking up molten metal souvenirs.'

Some families had property requisitioned for military use in the build-up to D-Day, and many soldiers from Scotland, Canada and finally America had the chance to enjoy home cooking once again.

From those school days, Jane and four others have kept in touch. In 1986 they held a reunion in Singleton for as many girls as they could muster. The five recently met again – and inevitably started to reminisce about the school staff.

Miss Ruth Matson was head; Miss Ogle was the school secretary; and the teachers included Miss Clarke and Miss Groome (history), Miss Payne (maths), Miss Crawley (French), Miss Muckle (art), Miss Millard (biology and science), Miss Cook (history) and Miss Childs (sport).

Keeping in touch with fellow pupils hasn't been so easy, though, for the obvious reason that marriage takes away a girl's surname. Judy Foster, Paddy Meaker, Marion Clemens and Margaret Hall all married and still live in Chichester. Ann Atkinson, Sheila Bradlaw, Mary Gough and Jane herself married, live in Surrey and still keep close links with Chichester.

Doreen Longhurst is in Leicester; Barbara King and Jacqueline Stephenson were last heard of somewhere in South Africa; and Gillian Ludlow lives in Johannesburg. Vivien Chapman used to be in Coombe Martin; two of the Fleming girls went to Australia, and another sister lived at Midhurst.

[27 January 2000]

Sharing with the Evacuees

June Arnold looks back fondly on her wartime childhood in Chichester – a childhood she shared with evacuees and their worldly-wise ways. Once, when her mother asked her where she'd been, she had to admit she'd been next door gambling with the evacuees. 'They had all learnt to play cards, and we were just greenhorns', Mrs Arnold recalls. 'But I think we all intermingled pretty well – though with the ones we had next door, the language was, shall we say, choice!

'I left school just as the war ended, so my schooling was basically right through the war. We shared our school with the evacuees. They had it for half a day and used the church hall for the other.

June Arnold and friends at a fancy dress party in the old council offices next to what is now Pallant House Gallery, c.1947.

A young June.

*A momentous day ...
it was second-hand,
but that didn't matter.
June becomes the proud
owner of her first bike
on her 13th birthday in
1943.*

'But they fitted in quite well. The whole thing ripped apart their families, though. I remember them all arriving with their gas masks waiting for people to take them, the poor things ... My mother couldn't take any because we had a smallish house and there were six of us in it already and we were bursting.'

As for the war itself, Mrs Arnold, of West Street, remembers her terror as the bombs dropped over Portsmouth: 'You could see the flames in the sky. My father used to put me under the stairs for safety ... I went with my mum and dad to Portsmouth once and they had all the barrage balloons up. I said "let's get the hell out of here and get back home!"' Otherwise, the war was simply something you accepted: 'You saw the dogfights overhead, the Spitfires and the Germans.'

'But I think the thing I was most aware of was the men in my family being sent away, my uncle, my cousin.' Her uncle survived Dunkirk and was then shipped out to Burma. Her cousin, an aircraft fitter, was sent out to Canada and subsequently emigrated there.

As for her father, he served in the 1914-18 war in Egypt and spent the Second World War in Chichester, managing Field's Garage in South Street.

'I was brought up on tales of Egypt', Mrs Arnold recalls. 'He [father] used to say how in Egypt the donkeys were overloaded, and the men used to slit the bags they were carrying to help them.'

Her father would also tell her of his fondness for the horse which saw him through the war. When the end came, the soldiers gathered to salute their horses out of respect and gratitude. 'He said he would have given anything to bring his horse home. It had carried him all through the desert.' Mrs Arnold's mother spent the First World War as a dietician looking after the wounded soldiers at Graylingwell, then a war hospital. 'My mother used to talk about Colonel Kidd who was the head of the hospital while she was there. She was working in the kitchen one day and he came up and said to my mother "you really shouldn't do your hair like that, it makes you too attractive!" She said that, otherwise, he was a very nice gentleman!

'Strangely enough, my mother died up there. She had come full circle.'

[24 September 1998]

No Mod Cons for Kate and her Nine Healthy Children

If you ever despair at the difficulties of looking after a baby, spare a thought for Kate Stubbs. Today's age of disposable nappies, wet wipes and cot monitors would seem a doddle to Kate, who raised nine children in an age when lighting was by gas lamp and when water had to be fetched.

Gladys King, who now lives in Chichester, was the eighth of nine children born to Kate and Arthur Stubbs in Midhurst between 1912 and 1933. Just five of them are still alive, but all of them survived infancy and childhood in good health. 'Those were the days when there was no hot water or central heating', Gladys recalls. 'There were no taps at the sink or anything. All the water had to be carried up from the pump.'

Kate was helped, though, in one respect. The First World War meant that she had effectively two families. The first children were born in 1912, 1913 and 1914, and the remaining six were born between 1920 and 1933, after Arthur's return from four years of fighting. The older children were able to help look after the younger ones.

Gladys' eldest sister, though, had grown up and left home by the time she was born, and Joan, the ninth and last in line, was in the curious position of becoming an aunt at the age of six months.

Gladys recalls: 'The Second World War started when I was nine. We had evacuees living with us for a time. It's just a dim memory now. And at one time we had children from Dr Barnardo's.

'My mother had a big family so they used to say to her "Come on, Mrs Stubbs, you can take a couple more children." We used to have to sleep top-to-tail in bed.

'There were three bedrooms. We had a big double bed in one room where the three girls used to sleep, and another single one in the same room. Later we had a small cot bed that Joan and I used to sleep in in mother's room.'

Surprisingly there were few disputes, and everyone got on well save for the odd family argument.

'We had a big common outside, being on a farm. We used to play bat and ball and hide and seek in the ferns. And we used to carry up about 20 to 30 buckets of water at the weekend so we could all have a bath on the Saturday night in front of the fire.' It was a case of youngest went first, with father topping up the water as the Stubbs family went – in age order – into the tub. 'Joan and I were the luckiest ones. We went in first!'

But despite the privations, the children all enjoyed good health. 'There were the usual things, mumps and chicken pox and one time Joan had glandular fever. But we were all pretty healthy.'

Under the watchful eye of their father, they grew up on the straight and narrow. 'I think he loved us all in his way, but he was very strict. He didn't like us to answer back and we weren't allowed to swear. If we picked up a swear word, we had a cuff around the ear pretty quick!'

[6 February 1997]

For Some Evacuees the Real Hardship came after the War

Pamela Burke looks back on the evacuation as a 'gigantic piece of super no planning', but she didn't regret it for a moment. It took her from an impoverished London background to the joys of West Wittering – such a liberation that returning home was a bigger wrench than leaving it. Looking back, Mrs Burke, who now lives near Reigate, vividly recalls the day West Wittering opened its arms and heart to a group of tired, bedraggled and awestruck children from Tooting. 'I know that my life was changed and greatly enriched from that day onwards.' The evacuation happened on 1 September 1939, two days before war was actually declared. It was a huge adventure.

'From my point of view as a poor London schoolchild, you didn't ever go away and if you did, it was with your parents. But we were going off on our own – no parents. I went with my sister.

'As I got older I thought how amazing the organisation was, but in fact they just stopped everyone from using public transport for three days. You had to be able to walk to a form of transport, and we went to a train station.

'Off we went in a crocodile. A train turned up and wherever that train was going was where you were going. It was not organised that such and such a school would go to such and such a place. It was a gigantic piece of super no planning.

'There was no question of "you can't get on that train because it's not going to West Wittering." The train came along, you got on it and you went to West Wittering because that was where the train was going.'

Mrs Burke, née Harris, was 11 at the time. She recalls it was an era well before the information explosion: 'You didn't know anything that was happening until you saw it in the newspapers in black and white the next day. There was no internet and all the other ways of getting information that you have today.'

But all of a sudden West Wittering was her home, and she stayed there for four and a half years. 'I went home for holidays, but I was basically down there for all that time, basically staying with two main people. The first was a single lady who I thought must be about 95 because she had silver hair, but in fact must have been about 48.

'She took in seven children and then she had to shift because her job was elsewhere. I then went and stayed with the billeting officer, a Mr Kewell. I was with him for three years and perhaps one year with the first lady. 'I knew them both until they died. They both came to my wedding. I went back to West Wittering church to get married.'

Mrs Burke remembers: 'I was extremely well treated. I was one of the people who benefited hugely from being evacuated. I went into quite a different level of society, and the two main people who looked after me were extremely kind. They were firm and all that, but they were very kind and I became extremely good friends with them – more than friends in fact, more like a second family.

'I just loathed going back to London. I just hated it. All the repercussions started. My family had said goodbye to an 11-year-old and got a 16-year-old back that had been living very independently. It was very difficult all round. There was no nastiness at the beginning, but there was at the end.'

Things resolved themselves, but it took time: 'We were used to going home on holidays so we didn't lose touch completely, but it was very difficult going home for real to a very war-scarred house, and it was very impoverished there. The war was over, but we were almost worse off for everything in some ways than while the war was happening. It took a good six years before you began to feel that things were getting easier.'

[3 February 2000]

Evacuee's Fond Memories of Chichester

Chichester became home for London lad Vivian Harris who was evacuated to the city for three years more than half a century ago. The recent VE and VJ 50th anniversary commemorations brought back memories of his adopted city for Mr Harris, who now lives in Walton-on-Thames.

On I September 1939 the Henry Thornton School at Clapham was evacuated, Mr Harris included. The boys were billeted in Bognor Regis and villages to the west including Rose Green and Pagham. Then it was found that there was no suitable school for them, so the boys were moved into Chichester where new billets were found. Arrangements were made for the school to share the building occupied by the high school for boys, a tight squeeze which required adjustments and compromises from all the parties concerned.

But whatever the discomforts, Mr Harris remembers the friendly welcome to this day.

'The people of Chichester who took us into their homes gave us shelter from the bombing attacks on the capital and I for one am eternally grateful to them. It must have been quite a problem for some of the hostesses who had to feed big lads of up to 18 years old on the few shillings' allowance. In addition some of the youth clubs welcomed us as members, notably those of the Congregational Church in South Street and St Paul's in Broyle Road.'

Vivian Harris, proud to serve in the Royal Sussex Regiment, April 1945.

It wasn't long, however, before Mr Harris and one at least of his chums were able to show their thanks by doing their bit for the war effort. 'In July 1940 when Anthony Eden broadcast an appeal for men to join the Local Defence Volunteers, later named the Home Guard, another evacuee and I put our age on and joined. For the next two years until I left school and Chichester, I was a member of the platoon led by Mr Leslie Evershed-Martin, who was later mayor and founder of Chichester Festival Theatre.

'Although I served four years in the Royal Sussex Regiment most of the time with the West African forces in India/Burma, I was never posted to Roussillon barracks in Chichester. But I have often returned to visit the city, which has a very special place in my memory and in my affections.'

[31 August 1995]

Taste of Awful School Dinners lingers on

Dennis Grainger and Dave Turner look back fondly on their days at Chichester's New Park Road Central School. Their days there spanned war and peace in the mid-1940s, but ask Dennis what he remembers most, and he'll screw up his face: 'Those awful dinners'. Momentous events were changing the course of history, but disgusting meals at school are Dennis' main memory. With Dave he would search out something more edible from the cake shop nearby.

They were happy days, he recalls. The teachers were pretty fair, even if one teacher did have a liking for hitting children with a ruler. 'She would hit you as many times as she liked. She would whack you in front of the class.' Dave remembers the offences could be as petty as eating or talking in class, trivial things which hardly warranted the beating. But otherwise lessons were fine. He particularly enjoyed reading Enid Blyton, reading which he considered safe.

As for Dennis he enjoyed arithmetic and English, and he reckons he learnt a lot, even if he says he's forgotten most of it since. Overall the feel of the school was quite jingoistic, Dave says: 'I can remember Empire

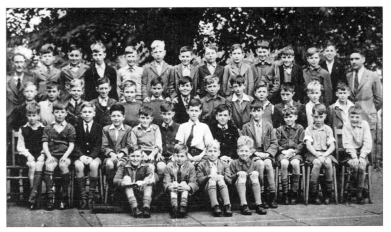

Right: *Central Boys'
School in New Park
Road, Chichester,
c.1946. Dave Turner is
fourth from the right
in the second row from
the back.*

Above: *A young Dave,
pictured in his 20s in
1953/4.*

Day. We would all have Union Jacks, and it was almost militaristic
marching around the playground.'

After the war came a period of austerity. The cessation of hostilities
brought few changes to the daily routine. 'A lot of teachers were coming
back out of the services just after the war, and I remember them as being
quite menacing. They would put great store by discipline as the most
appropriate way of bringing you up.'

Emotionally, it was a troubled time for many people, he recalls:
'Everybody came out of the war shell-shocked in some way ... Everybody
was coming back from the services. I know there were these wonderful
meetings between people, but relationships didn't grow again in the
ways they had done before the war – not that I remember that. I was too
young ... But things were certainly different. There was a lot of feeling
of alienation, and a lot of people having to adjust, a lot of people having
to look for work.'

Dennis remembers still the strange experience of seeing again the
father he hadn't seen for five years. 'I was about three when he went off
to war, and I was eight when he came back. I vaguely recognised him
when I saw him again, but it was very peculiar.'

As for Dave, the strangest meeting he recalls was when he saw his
first banana. 'I didn't know how to tackle it. It was the weirdest-looking
thing. The taste was extraordinary. I had heard about bananas. My mother
had said "Wait until the war is over and you can have a banana". It was
this great metaphorical carrot hanging there in front of me!'

[13 April 1995]

Rebel with White Drawers

Heather Ginman shudders even now at the thought of her worst moment
at school – the day she kicked the headteacher. Mrs Ginman joined
Chichester's Central Girls School in 1940 and blames her clean white
knickers for her day of shame. Clean white knickers might not sound
very much, but this was wartime. These were days of austerity; knickers
were regulation blue; Mrs Ginman was one of a large family; and these
were the days before washing machines.

'My mum put me in these white knickers and told me not to get them dirty. They had to last a week. We went for prayers at school in the hall and we were told to sit down, but I stood up because I knew that the hall would be dirty.

'I was told to sit down, but I said "I can't sit down because I have white knickers on". I was told to go to the front of the class. I thought I was going to be given a chair to sit on, but the teacher said "I am going to smack you for not sitting down". I said "If you do that, I am going to kick you". I am afraid she did and I did.

'I did feel awful about it. We had these heavy shoes on. It must have hurt. I was sent back to the classroom and that was my punishment – not to be allowed to sing in the hall. After that my mum told me to sit on the floor, despite my white knickers.' Mrs Ginman admits she was bit of a rebel: 'I was naughty, but I didn't see it as naughtiness. I saw it as just acting the fool.'

She also had a keen sense of what was wrong and what was right. The complete ban on associating with boys was utterly nonsensical in her view. 'I don't remember my first day at school exactly, but I had older sisters there so it wasn't a shock. The school was in Chapel Street then. But what I do remember is that we were not allowed to speak to the boys because it was considered disgusting. I was actually punished for walking to school with my brothers. I had to stand outside the headteacher's room every playtime for I don't know how long, but I am afraid I didn't stick to that. I ran away and took my sisters with me.' The war was on, and frankly there wasn't much the school could do. They wrote to her mother saying she'd been naughty, but Mrs Ginman's mother took her daughter's side on this particular one.

All in all, Mrs Ginman can't honestly say she enjoyed her school days. 'I didn't like the discipline. I have never been one for discipline even though I ended up a ward sister at Graylingwell. The discipline was just too strict. The bell would go at nine. You would be playing in the playground and you would have to stop instantly. The next bell would go and you would have to line up in twos for the classrooms. But if you were pushed or knocked by someone and you moved, you would get summoned to see the head. It was too much really.'

Even so, Mrs Ginman is prepared to let bygones be bygones and support the Central School Grand Reunion currently being planned. The Central Girls and Central Boys Schools grew out of the National Schools founded in Chichester in 1812. They both occupied several sites in the city, finally coming together in 1969 on the present site in Orchard Street. Many people still living in Chichester will remember with interest and affection – or perhaps even embarrassment and horror – their time spent in one or other of the schools. That's why the reunion is being planned.

[31 December 1998]

Whatever happened to the Boys from the Class of 45?

Michael Nieman chanced on his old school photo – and the memories started to pour back. Mr Nieman, who now lives in Gloucestershire, lived in Bognor Regis during the war and attended Chichester High School.

Form VM at Chichester High School for Boys, 1945/6. Michael Nieman is on the far right of the front seated row.

'I just came across this photo. I'm a collector of useless things, and you tend to remember the people you like. I suppose the point is that this photo of the class of 45 is a whole working lifetime away now and one wonders what happened to one's old classmates.' Mr Nieman is keen to chat again with old friends he hasn't seen for half a century, and he's hoping one or two might get in touch.

Mr Nieman joined the school in 1941, starting with the Henry Thornton School which was the evacuee school put with Chichester High. 'There wasn't room initially at the high school so that's where I started.'

There was no doubt there was a war on. 'Certainly one of the things I remember most was coming out of school one day, standing by the school gates and seeing parachutists coming down … Then we noticed it could only have been 100 foot above us – a bomber flying over the gates and it went straight into a factory, I think.'

The Liberator crashed, causing extensive damage on one of the blackest days wartime Chichester saw. 'I just remember a huge blast of heat. That was the main thing we felt – the tremendous heat.'

Another memory is of the day a Messerschmitt attacked the train on which he was travelling home to Bognor after school.

'It was machine-gunning the train. It wasn't very full at the time, but I just remember the orderly way we all got on to the floor. When we got out at Bognor, you could see machine-gun holes all down the side of the train.'

Mr Nieman doesn't remember the fear. He just remembers knowing what to do and doing it. 'I suppose if you are young during the war, you become immune to that kind of thing. You just grow up with it.'

As for the school, its head at the time was a Mr Bishop, Mr Nieman recalls – a quiet and good man. 'I also seem to remember that it was the first time we were having women teachers because the men were away fighting.'

Overall, it was a time of strong friendships, often struck up in the strangest of circumstances.

Mr Nieman recalls a tank crew which remained for a week or so outside their door in Bognor when Silverston Avenue was suddenly packed end-to-end with military hardware for the build-up to D-Day. Just as suddenly the tanks disappeared, and Mr Nieman never learnt the fate of the Canadian crew he had befriended.

But one way or another, he'd like to start renewing his links with his schooldays in wartime Chichester. 'A side effect of advancing years seems to be an increasing interest in what happened yesterday', he says.

[22 February 1996]

Children's Home Heartbreak

The strictest possible regime and stories to break your heart are a Chichester woman's memories of her work at a temporary wartime children's home near Chichester.

Hazel Barnett, née Wood, was a probationer nurse at the Dr Barnardo's home which was set up towards the end of the war.

'The children's home had been evacuated from London, and Lord Louis Mountbatten had, I think, given them permission to go to Adsdean House. I don't know how long for.

'But I remember it was all very strict. You had to be up at the crack of dawn. We were all young girls, and there were four of us sharing a room. I was terribly anxious because it was my first plunge into that kind of thing.

'We would all go down into a big dining room and eat as quickly as possible. When the matron or sister stood up, it meant that was it and we should go.

'One day a voice came down the table saying that there was a piece of toast on my plate and that I should eat it up because there was a war on. It was a big crime. It was wartime. They wouldn't tolerate any wastage.'

Standards were almost impossibly high. Mrs Barnett remembers scrubbing buckets until they were immaculately clean, but still being told to go back and do them again.

'There was no such thing as saying "Well done".'

On another occasion she found herself in the hottest of hot water. Her job was to bring the prams in from the balcony, but a nurse dragged her off insisting she was needed elsewhere. Mrs Barnett recalls trying to say that it was her job to bring the prams in, but her senior insisted she should leave it and that someone else would do it. 'At the end of the day I fell on my bed fully-clothed and then was shaken awake in the middle of the night and told to go down and finish the prams. Can you imagine anything like it these days? Boy, was I ticked off. I was carpeted completely.'

The children in the nurses' care were orphans or abandoned infants. Among them once was a black baby. None of the nurses had ever seen a black baby before.

'We were overwhelmed. I don't know where he had come from. We are going back 50 years now. He was so beautiful. I often think of him. We made much of him.'

A sadder memory is of a little child with a terrible condition which involved the softening of the bones: 'The poor little mite. When you picked it up, it was like a piece of jelly.'

Mrs Barnett's time at Adsdean House finished in similarly sad circumstances. She picked up an excruciatingly painful ear infection, and no one had any time to look after her. She remembers crawling along the corridor in terrible pain desperate to get a hot water bottle. Eventually her father came to find her after not hearing from her, but Mrs Barnett has no recollection of his arrival.

'The next thing I remember was that I woke up at the Royal West Sussex Hospital.'

The treatment involved hot compresses which would be smacked on her ear, but they worked in the end, and Mrs Barnett went back into nursing as a children's nanny in the United States.

[12 September 1996]

My Childhood Chums – the German POWs

Nigel Chitty remembers with affection the German prisoners-of-war who were his boyhood chums at North Mundham. Heinz Prime returned to Germany after the war but could not contact his family. He came back to North Mundham and then settled in Harrogate where he lived to a ripe old age.

But the prisoner named Paul went back to Germany never to return. He went to join his family in the east, and they were all shot by the Russians.

Nigel recalls: 'My mother bought him all the shaving stuff and soap when he went back to Germany. Heinz tried to contact him and found that he had been shot.'

The German PoWs came to North Mundham after the Allied D-Day build-up in the area had moved off for the Normandy landings and on into France. 'There were Italians and Germans and they stayed for some time after the war.'

The dark clouds of war seemed a long way away. Born in 1943, Nigel remembers that some of his earliest toys were made by the German PoWs. Nigel doesn't recall any great security surrounding them. 'When the crops were coming in we would get extra PoWs from the camp. I

Top: *Torox … helping to keep a nation healthy in wartime. An advertisement in the* Chichester Observer.

Below: *Beating flu … a wartime advertisement in the* Chichester Observer.

don't think at any time there would have been guards out there.

'I can remember my mother saying that they were all quite glad to be out of it. They were not young men. Heinz Prime was a farmer. He looked like he was in his 30s or 40s then. He was delighted to be out of the war.

'They used to say that they could have been on the Russian front. They were mostly captured in Normandy. We didn't think of them as the enemy.'

Nigel well remembers Heinz's broken English: 'There used to be a lot of pidgin English coming out, and we used to fall about laughing because he would recite little poems he had learnt to try to learn English.'

Nigel's memories are part of a heritage he keenly feels. He can trace his family back nine generations to a mayor of Chichester. His family first came to North Mundham Farm just before 1800. The family still live there now, and Nigel is working on various restoration projects which include the offices on site from which he is managing director of a company supplying technical products to pharmaceutical companies.

Look at him now

AND YET he was once so puny, so fretful and nothing would stay on his stomach. Then his mother tried Nestlé's Milk and, almost overnight, a change came about. Mother says Nestlé's was a'godsend. And all because Nestlé's Milk is rich, full cream country milk, Nature's own perfect food, so prepared that even a delicate baby can digest it easily.

Nestlé's Milk
RICHEST IN CREAM

Nigel remembers the days when North Mundham was just 20 houses and practically its entire population was closely connected to the land. Nowadays there are 200 houses.

'When a community loses its working places it just becomes suburbia. What we are trying to do is keep this working place alive.'

[31 October 1996]

Nestlé's Milk ... the recipe for wartime health. An advertisement in the Chichester Observer.

Chapter Five

WORK IN THE NEW ERA OF PEACE

The Man who taught the Duke to drive

There are now dozens of driving instructors serving the Chichester area. Once upon a time there was just one – Jack Miller. It was a long time ago, back in the days when a lady might spread a silk scarf across her knees for fear her instructor might notice them; back in the days when a novice might be taken for his first lesson to Chichester bypass as the easiest, straightest, quietest road to practise on.

Jack, now 87, started his motor school exactly 50 years ago this year. It's still going strong, now in the hands of his son, John. Jack was in the fire service in Portsmouth during the war. His parents had left him a house in Stockbridge Road. 'When I came out of the services, I thought I had better get a job,' he said.

During the war Jack had been in charge of the area driving school for the fire service's drivers and motorcyclists.

'So I went to Mason's garage which was in Southgate, and told him what I had been doing. I asked if there was a chance of a job teaching people how to drive – and stayed with him until 1949.'

The 'world's most exciting light car' arrives in Chichester in the 1950s. Jack Miller (right) is there to greet it.

That was the point at which he decided to go it alone. The driving test had been introduced in the 1930s, but was dropped in the early 1940s because of the war. It returned when the war was over. Jack said: 'I wrote for a job as a driving examiner. If I was going to go it alone, I needed petrol coupons. I applied for the coupons, and in the morning in the post came two letters. One was an appointment for driving examiners and the other was a whole batch of petrol coupons.

'I had to decide. My wife and I had a little confab and we set up Miller's Motor School. We had just one car.' Things developed, and after a while they leased the ground floor of 35 North Street. Jack's business developed to three or four cars.

Millers Motoring Academy adds to the fun of Chichester Gala during the 1950s. Jack, complete with cane and mortarboard, is the teacher.

'We had a big setback during the Suez crisis. That put a stop to things for the time being because there was no petrol. Driving tests were abandoned again. Learner drivers could drive unaccompanied. It completely wiped out the need for an instructor overnight.

'It lasted from November to May/June the following year. We struggled on somehow or other. I did a little bit of instructing if I could get the petrol.

'Having got over that, I heard that the lady who owned 57 North Street had died. To cut a long story short, we bought the premises and moved across here.'

It cost a princely £2,500, with a further couple of thousand on making it habitable. There wasn't even any electricity there. With time, Jack and John decided they didn't need a high street shop and so let the ground floor to a firm of estate agents who remain there to this day.

Over the years, the fundamentals of driving have remained the same, but driving today is most definitely not the same business as driving in Chichester half a century ago, Jack says. 'It was fairly quiet then. And driving around the Cross was easy!'

Jack is proud to have counted a number of distinguished learners among his clients. 'I taught Sir Anthony Eden's son. I also taught the present Duke of Richmond and I taught his brother. When I was at Mason's, that was when they first started the Goodwood circuit. I was instrumental in providing the first breakdown vehicle at Goodwood.

'I knew the old Duke, the present Duke's father, at the time. He was the one who really recommended me to people, and I taught a number of his staff. I had a very good connection with Goodwood at the time.'

These were the days when road rage was still a long way away. Plenty of patience was needed on the part of the instructor, but the learner could at least count on consideration from fellow road-users.

Now the speed, the density and the volume of traffic have changed things beyond all recognition. Tolerance for many has gone out the window, and aggression has increased. Jack is glad he's out of it now – left with happy memories of a gentler age.

[22 July 1999]

The Days when only Posh People had Cars

It will come as a surprise to most people strolling the streets of Chichester today that the city's first car park was in West Street, alongside the Cathedral.

The city's first car park attendant was First World War veteran William Walton, a man who went on to become the city's mace bearer for more than 20 years, a post he combined with that of town crier and hard-working custodian of the Assembly Rooms.

His daughter, Margaret Haylor, aged 70, remembers him as a lovely man. She is convinced hundreds of Cicestrians will remember him with similar affection. 'No one ever had a bad word to say against him.'

He was born, she believes, in India in 1898. His father was in the army and young William followed suit, putting on his age to serve in the First World War.

'They lived in Worthing then. He worked in a butcher's shop at 13 and then when he was 17 he went to France to fight … 'When he got there he met up with his father who said he was a "little fool" to come out. But he went right through the war. He served 12 years in the army in all. My mum and he were, I think, step-cousins. He had known her all his childhood and they were sweethearts. She was called Mabel Paine and she was from Chichester.' The couple lived in Orchard Street for more than 40 years.

'When dad came out of the army, mum worked for a Dr Buckle in Lion Street. She used to be a maid and they used to have guests there. There was a chap from the council. Mum said dad was coming out of the army. Jobs were pretty hard to get in those days. This man told her there was a car park attendant needed.' The car park was right next to the Cathedral, and a treasured photograph shows Mr Walton on duty (see p.60).

Margaret Haylor as a toddler in her mother Mabel's arms. Also pictured is Margaret's brother William.
The photograph was taken in Franklin Place, Chichester, c.1930.

These were the days when only posh people had cars, Mrs Haylor recalls: 'They mostly had chauffeurs, and they would bring my dad apples and rabbits and pheasants. … He only earned the equivalent of £2.50 a week, working from nine in the morning until six at night seven days a week. We were hard up, really hard up, not like people are today. … The parking was sixpence a day. My father used to bring back his book of tickets and save his money and take it once a week to the council.'

Her father's work at the car park provides some of Mrs Haylor's earliest memories. 'There were gates to the Cathedral, I remember, and these gates were locked at night. We used to go and meet Dad and see the gates being locked and the old lamplighters coming.'

Mr Walton was still working there when the Second World War came. In fact, he was caught in West Street when Chichester was bombed. One bomb came down behind Woolworth's; another ended up in St Martin's Street. Mr Walton took cover behind the trees as the machine-gun bullets rained down.

William Walton
– the city's first car
park attendant. He is
pictured outside the
cathedral just before
the Second World War.

'After that he was going to join the army, but the council said no, there was an important job they wanted him to do down at Florence Road, being in charge of all the salvage down there. ... They had it as a tip. They then started baling up all the paper and keeping all the bottles and everything separate. He was there until after the war when the council said he had done a good job and would he like to keep it. He said no. ... He was a really lovely man. Loads of people are bound to remember him and say how nice and obliging he was and always polite.

'He was a lovely father. He would have Thursday afternoon off. He had bought us bikes. On Thursdays he would go to the cake shop and buy four French loaves and half a pound of butter, and we would go off to Goodwood on his half-day out.'

It was during the war that Mr Walton took on the duties of mace-bearer. To these were added the duties of town crier. The appointment letter expresses the hope that the happy day might not be so very far off when as town crier Mr Walton would proclaim peace to the city.

Mrs Haylor remembers her father took his duties very seriously. He kept the Assembly Rooms spotless and put in an incredible number of hours – the equivalent of 12 hours a day seven days a week. If something was happening at the Assembly Rooms, he had to be there.

If there was a party or a dance which went on until four in the morning, Mr Walton would think nothing of kipping down on the floor for a couple of hours before starting work at seven. Sadly he was not to see a long retirement. 'Having worked hard all his life, he retired in 1963 and died just three years later.'

[12 August 1999]

Force was with Archie

Getting locked in a cell with a suicidal prisoner and getting arrested as a suspected flasher were just two of the scrapes Archie Greenshields got into in his 26½ years as a Sussex policeman.

Top: *Winners of the police first aid cup at Littlehampton in 1950. Left to right, back row, Archie Greenshields, Sgt Kennett, and front row, PC Stear, PC Taylor and PC Dale.*

Above: *PC Archie Greenshields goes on patrol with his trusty bike and mackintosh at Rustington, 1951-2.*

Archie joined up in 1946 at a time when East and West Sussex constabularies were still separate. In the years that followed, he served in a succession of locations including Bognor Regis – where he still lives – Chichester, Worthing, Petworth and Rustington.

Archie, now 78, was born on the site which is now Chichester's library – one of six children in a little house with a shared toilet and one tap. It was knocked down in the slum clearance after the war, by which time Archie was embarked on his police career.

'The training was rough. I broke my arm during the physical training. Another chap had his eye gouged out with a loose lace from a boxing glove. Another one had a broken leg. There were three of us there all crippled. They always seemed to put the biggest with the littlest for the unarmed combat!'

One of the challenges was to learn to swim, something he managed eventually, but not before his first posting – next to the second fastest-flowing river in England. 'I used to walk past the river as quickly as I could! ... For two or three years I was at Littlehampton and then I went to Rustington as a rural beat officer. My twin daughters were born there.

'All policemen's wives in the country were invaluable to the force. They took the messages and passed them on to their husbands on the beat. Remember, in those days you didn't have radios. We just had telephone boxes. We made conference points at a telephone box or other likely places. You would wait there for five to ten minutes to see if there was a message and then continue to your next one.'

His next posting was Worthing where he suffered the indignity of being arrested by his new colleagues. 'I was put on observation duties. There was an outbreak of indecent exposure in the road that had a private girls school in it. The private girls school had an annexe. While I was on observation for this man who was doing it repeatedly, I kept observation from this steamroller that was there. ... But I was not too sure where the last offence had taken place. In the distance I saw a member of the staff come out from one part of the school. As she neared, I got out of my observation point and went to ask her.

'But before I had the chance, she attacked me with an umbrella and was shouting "Go away, you filthy beast!" I said "I am a police officer", but she didn't take any notice. She went off and called the police. I knew I was in trouble. I had only recently gone to Worthing. There were at least a hundred policemen, and I didn't know them all.

'Within a minute or two, a van arrived. They got hold of me. They wouldn't listen when I said I was a policeman. Unfortunately I hadn't got my warrant card with me. I had a red face.'

From Worthing he was posted to Petworth and from Petworth to Bognor where his adventures reflected him in a rather better light. 'I was the station officer on one particular night. I was warned that there was a man in the cell when I came on duty. We are required to visit a prisoner in a cell at least once an hour. I went down to the cell and I

Archie, in a white smock, joins in the fun for the Petworth police pantomime, Christmas 1961. Father Christmas is Superintendent Doney.

said to the man "You had better make your bed up". I said I would come back in a little while.

'All he had was a wooden bed and a mattress and two blankets. Before the hour had elapsed, I went down to fulfil my promise only to find he had ripped the side of the mattress right the way around, taking the plastic covering off.

'He had tied it to the ventilation flaps in the cell window, had put it round his neck and had jumped off the bed. I opened the cell and took the strain. I cut the plastic with a small knife that I had in my pocket and he fell back, knocking me back. I hit the door of the cell and it slammed to.

'I wasn't too worried at that stage because the man was unconscious. I gave him mouth to mouth. I gave him first aid. Eventually he started to splutter. He foamed and everything came out of his mouth. He started to breath erratically, and then my problem was to get out of the door.

'I could not reach the key that was still in the place outside. I was the only officer there. The rest were on patrol. I rolled up what was left of the mattress and eventually managed to reach the key and get out.

'I got the message out to send help to Bognor station. I went back and tried to get sense out of the man. Within a couple of minutes people started to arrive. An ambulance was called and he was sent off to hospital under guard.

'I don't know what happened to him. I had saved his life, but I don't know what became of the man.'

[20 May 1999]

Company Boss Started at Bottom when he was Eight

Frank Burden was just eight when he first started working for Chichester builders Frederick Hill Ltd.

Nearly 70 years later and now chairman of the company, he looks back fondly on those early-morning pre-school starts. 'I used to start at 7am, sweeping out the offices and doing the dusting and the cleaning. For that I had a shilling a week out of which I had to give my mother sixpence for my keep.'

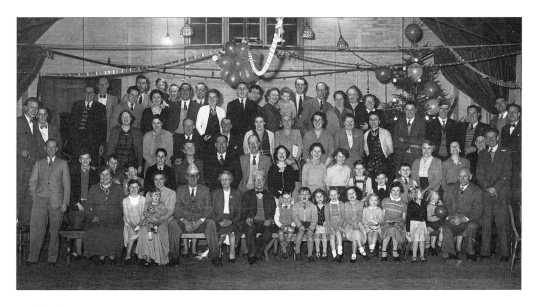

Works Christmas party, 1954. Frank Burden is on the extreme right. His father is in the centre of the front row.

Frederick Hill was started by Mr Hill in 1898 in Northgate and during the early years of the century the company built, among others, the large Edwardian houses on the north side of The Avenue.

It was around that time that Mr Burden's father Henry joined the firm, taking shares in it and then taking over with a Mr Rines when Mr Hill retired in the early 1920s. Mr Hill kept up his interest, popping in from time to time, but sadly Mr Rines was forced out of action with creeping paralysis, and chief clerk Mr Arnell took his place.

Back in those days, the works annual outing was an eagerly-anticipated event and Mr Burden junior used to be the mascot for the day.

'They would go to Bristol or Bath or Cheddar Caves or places like that and there were always crates of beer on board the charabancs. ... I always remember that they would stop on the way to the various places and they would draw a chalk line on the road. They used to throw pennies to see who could get closest to the line. The person who was closest would win all the pennies.'

The games were simple, and so were the working methods. These were the days when the timber had to be delivered from Littlehampton and would then be taken out of the yard by horse and cart. Even to outlying areas, horse and cart was the only way of getting tools and materials on site. Mr Burden remembers one occasion when a ladder was taken down to the Witterings on a push cart. On arrival it was found to be too short and had to be pushed all the way back again.

Once he'd completed his schooling, Mr Burden went to work in Dorking and it wasn't until after the war that he went back into the family business.

One change he instituted was that the works outings were replaced by Christmas parties, each with a different theme. One year Father Christmas would come down a replica chimney; another year he would arrive by sleigh. One year, marking the dawn of the space age, he arrived by Sputnik. Or a replica Sputnik, to be more precise.

63

But it wasn't all fun in the immediate post-war days. Much of the work was rebuilding work, clearing away bomb-damaged properties. About ten years after the war, the number of staff rose to an all-time high of around 70 to keep up with the demands of peace-time building.

Now, just a couple of years away from its centenary, Frederick Hill Builders are still going strong. Changing times and different demands meant they recently left behind their Northgate premises in favour of a site in Apuldram Lane South. But the family tradition remains as strong as ever. Pictures of those Christmas parties 40 years ago show a little boy on a lap. That boy is Jeremy Burden, present managing director.

[27 June 1996]

No Regrets about a Life spent working with Wood

Ask Frank Hellyer his religion, and he says it's his job. Ask him his job, and he'll just say wood. For all his working life except a six-week mistake right at the start, 67-year-old Frank has devoted himself to the timber trade. By eight years he's the longest-serving member of staff at Covers, and he's got no intentions of retiring. He's looking forward to Covers' 150th anniversary celebrations next year. And so he should. He's been with the company for comfortably half a century.

Wood is Frank's hobby, his work and his life, but back in the early 1940s it took him six weeks as an apprentice plumber to realise it. 'I left school when I was 13 and always wanted to be a plumber', says Chichester-born Frank. 'I started work with Frederick Hill's, the local builders, but after six weeks I realised I didn't want to be a plumber. 'My father said to me "You aren't very happy, are you?" Then he said to me something that was very profound. He said "if you don't like what you're doing, don't do it – you'll never be any good at it".'

Frank resigned and started work in The Hornet with Kenneth Long's, a company that had been bombed out of London and directed to Chichester. It was his first step in the timber trade and a big step towards Covers

Sales rep Sam Weller lends a hand with the heavy work in the Hornet, c.1948/9.

Frank Hellyer working with wood in 1950, having started work with Covers in February 1942.

who bought the premises and the business in the early 1950s when Long's went back to London.

Covers, by then already more than 100 years old, was based at the Canal Basin. Its expansion into The Hornet allowed the staff numbers to go up from 20 to about 60.

It began a chapter in the company's history which has seen it become a chain with nine outlets ranging from Gosport to Bognor Regis, from Portsmouth to Brighton, and with a staff of around 230 at its Chichester site, now in Quarry Lane.

Over the years, Frank has been successively labourer, yard supervisor, yard foreman, mill foreman, general manager and production manager, and now director and general manager. During that time he's seen the advent of computers and a massive increase in feed speeds on machinery, huge advances in mechanical handling and the arrival of the forklift, a simple device which has revolutionised the timber trade.

In days gone by, it would take three hours to unload a lorry. Now it can be done in ten minutes. Back then, every piece of timber had to be handled one by one. Now it comes in packs, and the work is far less back-breaking.

But of all Frank's memories, the one that stands out most is the day the Liberator came down in Chichester. The American bomber crashed within 50 yards of where Frank was working at Long's. It skimmed over the allotments and crashed into the electric laundry. 'I didn't see it at all. I just heard this bloody great bang and saw a flash. It was all burning and going off bang.'

Then just 16, Frank still remembers the crew, who had parachuted out, coming back that night to survey the devastation. 'All up in the trees around the site there were bits and pieces of plane. It's the kind of thing that you remember.'

[28 September 1995]

The 'Unseen City' beneath our Feet

Builder Harold Vivash well remembers the day he suddenly found himself standing in Chichester's vast underground city. Chichester's late Victorian drainage system is a sight seen by few people, but it became a focus for debate during last year's flooding. What was its extent? Could it be revived to form an effective flood relief system? How do you get into it?

For Mr Vivash, the answer to the last at least of these questions couldn't possibly have been more prosaic. His access proved to be through a lavatory. Mr Vivash, aged 73, of Lewis Road, recalls: 'I once worked for Mr Clemens, a good builder, and on one occasion I had the job of replacing a WC pan in an outdoor lavatory which was behind the boot repair shop that stood in the Bottleneck at Westgate. 'I had started to cut out the old pan from the floor. I stopped for tea. When I returned, the pan had disappeared into a hole. I looked into this hole but couldn't see the pan, and reaching in as far as I could I couldn't feel anything. … I had to go back to the works for a ladder so that I could get down into the hole. It was a chamber, about eight and a half feet deep, six feet wide and 12 feet long.

'At each end there was an oval outlet about three feet high. The opening at the north end came from the back of Orchard Street. And there was yet another system of similar size which joined the Lavant to the above chamber in another direction. ... Both chambers were well constructed of brick. When the Westgate roundabout was built, they were filled with clay and rubble and forgotten. But in one of them, you could have nearly driven a double decker through.'

Mr Vivash's time in building came after a spell serving his country. He'd upped his age and joined the Navy as soon as he could in 1940. After ten weeks training at HMS *Collingwood* in Fareham, he joined HMS *Fury* for service in the Mediterranean and on the Atlantic convoys. On one occasion he was up in the crow's nest and saw a torpedo heading towards the ship. He alerted the captain and the ship pulled hard to starboard, averting disaster.

On another occasion, Mr Vivash was up in his crow's nest when he found 37 Italian bombers heading towards him. Their machine guns ripped through the funnels, and Mr Vivash had just canvas to protect him.

Mr Vivash came out of the Navy in 1946 and concluded his working life with 23 years with the city council. But even now he retains particularly fond memories of his Chichester school days more than 60 years ago. He recalls the time as an era of great discipline but equally great freedom. Shoes which were less than shiny and punctuality which was less than spot-on brought swift and painful punishment, but at least children were safe to roam the streets and picnic where they liked.

Mr Vivash recalls vividly rolling iron hoops along the street on his way to school, not a car in sight. 'It's changed a bit since those days!'

[21 September 1995]

Alf's Crowning Glory

A shin-high Chichester city centre tribute to royalty goes unnoticed by thousands of people each day. But for city bricklayer Alf Butler it would probably be satisfaction enough to just to know that it's still there. Nearly half a century after he created it, his light-hearted coronation commemoration has so far stood the test of time.

Alf's daughter-in-law Iva Butler is one of probably just a handful of people who know where to find it. At the bottom of a wall opposite the funeral director's in South Pallant, it's plain to see – if you know where to look. Look hard and you'll see the shape of a crown built into the brickwork.

Alf was a jovial old chap, Mrs Butler recalls. 'He was a bricklayer. They were all in the building trade. And there was plenty of sense of humour in him. He was a great character really.'

Mrs Butler, with her two young children, was round at her mother-in-law's on the day of Queen Elizabeth II's coronation in 1953. As a young mum, she didn't have time to celebrate too much, but she remembers well enough watching the coronation on the television. 'It was just black and white, but it was still exciting. I love the uniforms and all that. I like pomp and circumstance. When they used to have carnivals, and you'd see the bands in their uniforms, I'd always have a lump the size of a football in my throat.' And Coronation Day was no different.

Above: *Alfred Butler, loyal bricklayer, pictured in the 1940s in Chichester.*

Right: *Iva Butler and her husband Jack pictured at Arundel in 1947.*

She felt moved by it all, and so too did her father-in-law. When he came home from work, Mrs Butler was delighted to discover that Alf had paid a little tribute on behalf of all of them.

'He wasn't a big royalist, I shouldn't have thought. But I suppose it was an event that was happening and he thought he wanted to do something about it. It was an inspiration sort of thing.'

Mrs Butler originally came from Portsmouth, and it was thanks to the war that she found herself in the Chichester area. 'We were bombed out and came to Bognor. We stayed with my uncle in Sudley Road to start off with. ... Our house in Portsmouth wasn't bombed, but there was an unexploded bomb a few yards from us. We lived opposite Fratton Park football ground. It was the last raid that they had on Pompey. St Mary's Hospital was hit with incendiaries, and so was Fratton Park. ... We were only two families, us and the Broadbridges, left in the road at the time. My father was working in the dockyard and so was the other man, Mr Broadbridge, when the bomb came down. They were both on duty. There was just my mother and Mrs Broadbridge.'

Mrs Butler's mother didn't want to leave, but the war had come too close. ... 'And so we came to Bognor.' ... The family moved several times in the town, but in the meantime Mrs Butler had met her husband, Jack, and moved to Chichester.

[25 February 1999]

Royal Seal of Approval

What would Herbert Willard make of it now, one wonders.

He started out in the 1920s doing part-time work building radio sets. 70 years later, the company he founded is one of the world's leaders in the production of art conservation equipment. What's more, as of this year, his company is 'by Royal appointment to the Queen'.

Chichester-based Willard Developments has received a Royal Warrant – the latest chapter in a remarkable story of success.

The warrant recognises the role the company played in the aftermath of the disastrous fire at Windsor Castle. But their wider role has been a truly global one. There probably isn't a major art gallery in the country which hasn't got a piece of Willard equipment, and their list of overseas clients is impressive in the extreme.

The company can truly claim to be pioneers. They set the parameters and led the way. And now they come with Royal approval. Herbert's son Jack believes his dad would be rather chuffed. 'In the really early days he was building the radio sets, but in about 1930 he decided to move on', Jack recalls. 'The radio sets had got commercialised by then. There were a dozen or more radio firms that had set up, so he decided to specialise in electrical contracting because of all the house-building that was going on. ... We wired all over Parklands in Chichester. He also wired nearly all of Rose Green and Pagham.'

As a young lad, Jack started to do bits and pieces for his dad, but it wasn't until after his apprenticeship in Portsmouth and three years in the Navy that he joined the family firm. It was Willard Electrical at the time, but by 1971 the art conservation equipment side had grown to such an extent that Jack and his father, shortly before Herbert's death, set up Willard Developments, specifically for the art side of the business.

Jack Willard, of the middle Willard generation, pictured in the 1950s.

Jack recalls: 'It really started in about 1950 when a student from the Courtauld Institute brought in a piece of conservation equipment that

Company founder Herbert Willard with works foreman Jack Luke, pictured in the 1960s in Leigh Road, Chichester, where the company remains to this day.

had just been knocked up, really. It was pretty rough and lethal really. It was a heated spatula of a sort – a flat surface of metal that had been screwed into a chisel handle. It had a piece of tube welded on with a little element with just wires running up. ... It was most unsatisfactory. I said "I could make something much better if you were interested". And that created quite a stir. None of the museums or art galleries got anything made by an engineering firm back then. It was just conservators building equipment themselves, stuff that was invariably pretty dangerous from the point of view of no proper heat control or just very poor heat control.'

These days, thanks largely to Willard, art conservation equipment is highly specialised and highly high-tech. Back then, conservation departments were basically a series of benches with pictures lying around on them, Jack says.

Ordinary domestic irons had been tinkered with to become heating tools, but it was rudimentary stuff.

Jack took the trouble to find out what the Courtauld wanted, and he took the trouble to make it specifically for them. Other galleries were soon and understandably interested.

'The V&A followed closely on their heels when they heard that somebody was going to make these tools, followed by the Tate and the National Gallery. They were very pleased with what they had got. Basically, it just needed someone with an electro-mechanical background to pioneer these one-off pieces for them.' It took a particular approach and skill, Jack recalls – the ability on his part to determine what the galleries needed, to sketch it out quickly, to design it, to work out the parameters and to go off and make it.

And that's precisely what he did …

[31 January 2002]

Door-to-Door for 38 Years

At 82, Roy Stenning pampers himself a little. He works just a couple of hours a day and doesn't range quite as far afield as he once did. But ask him whether retirement is on the cards, and he'll throw up his hands in horror.

He's one of the longest-serving independent Kleeneze agents in the country and possibly the oldest, and it's not a job he'll give up lightly. With 38 years to his credit, he's looking forward to quite a few more years yet. He's enjoying it as much as ever.

Born in Chichester in the year of the Battle of the Somme, Mr Stenning worked first for a firm of solicitors. He then went into his father's cycle business, but by the late 1950s, with two growing sons to support, he became a Kleeneze agent.

A familiar face and a familiar van … Roy Stenning, who has given years of Kleeneze service. He is pictured in the summer of 1973.

He took to the deliver-to-your-door household goods trade well: 'I eventually ran a group of up to around 30 agents as far as I can remember.'

Life was certainly varied. On one occasion he was left looking after a baby being bathed in a sink while its mother went upstairs to find some money. On two occasions he found himself in a house with a mentally-deranged person and couldn't help wondering how he would effect his escape.

But the overwhelming majority of his customers, he says, have been a joy to do business with. 'In all my years I think I have come across unpleasant people maybe six or seven times. I remember one man marched me down to the gate and more or less shooed me off the premises. I called on the lady next door to him. I knew her and she told me she had had a lot of trouble with this particular person. There were always fights between him and his wife. I felt a little bit better. It was not just me he was antagonistic to!'

Another scrape was at the barracks: 'I had a pass to go to the people living in the barracks. I went in one day and a chap with a gun accosted me. He wouldn't take what I told him to be the truth. He marched me across the quadrangle to the adjutant who then roundly told him off. He was most embarrassed.'

Roy Stenning, a salesman convinced that a smile always wins. The photograph was taken by a customer who was trying out a new camera.

But these are the exceptions. Throughout his working life, Mr Stenning has found that courtesy and pleasantness have almost invariably been repaid in kind. 'When I first started, they used to tell me that the first thing for a salesman to sell is himself. I could not make out what on earth they meant, but I learnt that if you are pleasant to people they respond in the same way.'

Supported by his wife Mary, Mr Stenning consequently came up with good sales figures, and in recognition attended Kleeneze conferences – semi-holidays which allowed sight-seeing and time-off – in a string of UK locations, from Bristol to Brighton and from Eastbourne to Buxton.

He also attended Kleeneze conferences in Portugal, Spain, Tenerife, Rhodes and Jersey – all at the company's expense. Such trips aren't possible any more, but Mr Stenning is as determined as ever to keep up his good work.

[24 June 1999]

Chapter Six

SCHOOLING IN THE POST-WAR WORLD

Sunday School Fun at Portfield Hall

Sunday School in post-war Chichester was a happy feature of Everil Hole's week.

Mrs Hole, of Royal Close, was born in Chichester in 1941 and, not surprisingly, remembers little about the war itself – except that she used to sing in the air-raid shelter to help keep spirits up.

More concrete are her memories of her days at the Portfield Sunday School which she joined soon after peace returned to the city. Children would meet at the Portfield Hall (now houses) and then go for prayers at the church which is now the mechanical toy and doll museum. It was all good fun, she recalls.

'We used to go to Hayling Island on a Sunday School outing every year. We used to have a coach down there and we used to mainly stay on the beaches. We used to take our sandwiches and it used to be a real treat. I remember there was a small fun fair there.'

Other institutions which loomed large in Mrs Hole's young life included the fire brigade for which her father was a transport officer. Mrs Hole has fond memories of the fire brigade Christmas parties from the time when the fire station was in Market Avenue. 'The firemen used to make toys out of wood for us. Most of the toys were hand-made. They used to clear the fire engines out and the party was where the fire machines had been. The floor was all oily, and they used to put sawdust down to keep the oil at bay. I can still see the sawdust now.'

As for other social events, it was back to Portfield Hall, scene of Sunday School. 'They used to have whist drives and so on there, organised by Mr Dowling. He used to arrange them and he used to rent the hall. They used to have huge big prizes like chicken and fruit and flowers and all sorts of things. ... They used to have social evenings there. The vicar of Portfield used to come in and we would have games and dances. It was long before television was in, and it was a nice place to go. ... The place was closed in the end for quite a while and then was turned into housing, though they kept part of the shape of the building.'

[21 March 1996]

Memories of Old-Style Nursery School

Not many mums and dads these days would tolerate their children being put down for a sleep every afternoon at nursery school. But things were different back in 1954 when Natalie Fuller became a trainee nursery nurse.

Children these days tend to do just a few sessions a week at pre-school or nursery.

Back in the 1950s, the hours were much, much longer. The children would attend five days a week, nine to four. In the middle of the day they had a cooked meal, prepared on the premises. No wonder the children needed their nap ... Mrs Fuller started her training at Chichester Nursery School and qualified in 1957. Now retired, she went on to enjoy a fulfilling career working with children.

When she first went there, Chichester Nursery School was in the old Henty building in College Lane. 'When Mrs Henty died, she left the building in her will to the county. The top half was used for civil defence. The nursery school had the bottom half.'

Mrs Fuller admits she didn't have a yardstick to judge it by, but she was definitely impressed. 'They were beautiful old rooms, and there was masses of space for the children. But there were lots of things, I suppose, that they wouldn't get away with now. There was an enormous lake at the bottom of the garden, just kept separate by a picket fence. Ofsted would go into overdrive if they saw that now!

'But the rooms were beautiful. And after lunch every day, the children were put down for a sleep for about an hour. They were there from nine in the morning. Half of them weren't collected until four. There weren't many cars in those days. The mothers would be trudging up the hill with their children. And so most of the children needed their sleep in the afternoon!'

Woodlands Children's Home Christmas party in 1958. Natalie Fuller is in black, seen in profile in the middle.

Party time at the nursery school in the 1960s.

The sleep wasn't always undisturbed. 'As a student, one of my earliest memories was having to scrub down the beds after the children had had accidents.' It was all part of a disciplined regime. There were standards of dress for the staff and clear do's and don'ts, but Mrs Fuller, who lives just opposite the Festival Theatre, doesn't look back on it as strict in the strict sense of the word. 'Strict isn't the word I would use. I think it was more that the children knew what was expected and they knew where to stop, which I don't think is always the case nowadays.

'I spent most of my nursery school time at Chichester Nursery School. I have worked with children all over the place, but I do think that the Chichester Nursery School was a very caring sort of place. The staff always cared about what they were doing, and the children always came first. As one of the students, I knew that the children's interests were always first and that everything was done for the children's comfort.'

Of course, it's a different place now, but no less caring. There is now more by way of equipment; there are greater opportunities for the children; and there is now much more by way of parental involvement.

'Perhaps because I was bottom of the ladder then, I remember that the parents just seemed to be in quite a hurry to drop the children off and then collect them. When I was at the nursery school last week looking at old photos, I found it wonderful that the parents were coming in and getting involved. There is a lot more working together than there used to be.'

[20 December 2001]

School's Legacy lives on 300 Years later

The year 2002 will be the 300th anniversary of the founding of the Oliver Whitby School in West Street, Chichester. And though the school closed on December 21 1949, the remarkable Oliver Whitby legacy continues still, in the form of the Oliver Whitby Educational Foundation which funds pupils to this day at Christ's Hospital, near Horsham.

Oliver Whitby died at the age of just 39, but in his will – written with the knowledge of approaching death – he ensured that his name at least lives on.

Peter Hughes (old boy 1945/49) is now working to ensure that the full history will be told for the tercentenary year with the publication of a special commemorative book. It is a project which has certainly stirred plenty of memories.

The school closed, Peter recalls, because the national educational system was now offering a better education than the education the school offered. 'The Oliver Whitby School was seen as something of a dinosaur in that era just after the war. It was a boarding school and it was a charity school.

'The story is that Oliver Whitby was the son of the Archdeacon of Chichester. Just before he died, he left a will in which he left money for the education of 12 poor boys to be taken from Chichester, Harting and West Wittering.'

The terms of the will were very specific. These three locations were places where the family owned farmland and property, and these were the places from which the funds for the school were to be generated.

73

This was the way many educational establishments were founded before being brought together under national co-ordination.

'The difference between Oliver Whitby and the others was that it was a boarding school. The poor boys would be kept and fed and housed as well as educated.' Peter admits that not much is known about Oliver Whitby himself, but it wasn't until ten years after its founding that the school, with its distinctively-clad blue-cloaked pupils, was ready to open. By then, the trustees had accumulated sufficient funds to obtain a property and appoint suitable staff.

Peter recalls his days there as rather tough: 'It was a harsh regime. Your time was very heavily controlled. You got up in the morning, you washed and then you had to do jobs before breakfast. ... The two jobs that I was particularly connected with while I was there were polishing the fine oak staircase, which is still in storage in the A&N store, and cleaning the bathrooms. We had two baths. There were 42 boys while I was there. I used to clean the baths every day. ... And we used to clean them with brick dust. Vim and things like that were not brought into the school. We used to scrape the brick dust from the bricks in the garden. It wasn't easy, but you just accepted it.'

Peter wasn't impressed by the standards of education either: 'The education was very basic. I would not say that it was bad. But I don't think it broadened the mind enough. I tend to feel that it was lacking. It covered all the rudimentary subjects. RI was very much an important area – also maths, algebra, geometry, composition, English and so on.

'But it didn't really bring you up to really good O-level standard. I don't think it came up to a sufficient standard in the end.'

[9 August 2001]

Knickers, Peaches and Life in a Fifties' Girls School

Audrey Evans' knicker linings had one leg six inches longer than the other. Blood from pricked fingers stained the seams. So the six per cent she got in her sewing exam was probably a fair reflection of her talents. Even so, she looks back fondly on her Chichester schooldays. Now Audrey Willis, she joined the Girls High School at the age of ten in 1936.

She lived at The Peacheries on the Bognor Road, and there her father, as had her grandfather before him, grew a wide range of fruit and veg under glass. Her father sold up in about 1950. 'The bottom dropped out of the peach market when they started selling lots of peaches brought in from other countries', Mrs Willis recalls. 'English peaches were grown at great expense under glass, and you couldn't compete.' The Chichester peaches would be sent off to Covent Garden and would supply the best hotels in London. Her father also grew mushrooms and lettuces.

Audrey Evans, aged 14, in summer school uniform.

Left: *The girls of the Girls' Training Corps, pictured in Chichester in 1941. From left to right, Peggy Fogden, Jill Dawe and Audrey Evans.*

One result was that Mrs Willis never remembers going hungry during the war. In fact the war didn't trouble her a great deal, she remembers – even if it did mean nights spent under the shelter of the kitchen table while bombs rained down on neighbouring Portsmouth. 'My memories of wartime are very clear. I remember thinking it was not worth working as I might be killed with a bomb at any time.'

It was also a time of great friendships. 'Sue Marmont, Helen Fleming and I were games cupboard monitors manning the games cupboard and giving out equipment which had to be signed for at break and dinner hours.'

Mrs Willis has kept a diary for most of her life, and she was looking through the entries for the 1950s the other day and found Helen's wedding photograph. It certainly stirred memories – all the more so perhaps for the fact that Mrs Willis moved away from Chichester at the age of 15.

Life was full, very full. As a result, she didn't keep up many of her Chichester contacts – something she is hoping to correct now in later life. The memories are certainly vivid enough – dark air-raid shelters, candles, quizzes, and Marion Clemens' drawing skills.

'We had many lessons at the Bishop's Palace after Streatham High School joined us.'

It wasn't necessarily conducive to work. Mrs Willis recalls that the hot garden was total bliss for a dreamer such as she. But much of the teaching clearly got through.

'I have much to thank Miss Groom for. Her inspired teaching of English literature is responsible for my poetry writing today. ... Another happy memory – the direct result of Streatham High School coming to Chichester – was the arrival of Miss Lombard, a gifted teacher of dance.'

[23 March 2000]

Do the Boys from the Class of '61 still dress like Elvis?

Sheila Francis admits she wasn't exactly a model pupil and there were certainly times when she wasn't there when she should have been. But she'd still love to meet up once again with anyone who shared her schooldays (and her love of Elvis) at Manhood School between 1959 and 1961.

Sheila and friends are planning a reunion at Sidlesham Football Club, an idea which took shape after a surprise birthday party for a fellow ex-pupil earlier this year.

The party set them thinking that it would be rather nice to relive those days – and to see whether the boys still look like Elvis. These were the days when a new Elvis film was a big event and when playing truant seemed a reasonable way to pass the day, she recalls.

'I grew up in Sidlesham but I went to Selsey school. I joined in 1959 at the age of 11. It was Selsey Secondary Modern School back then and it was very disciplined. ... It was a big school and we were very wary of the teaching staff, but we respected them, and among the pupils there was a friendly atmosphere.'

Sheila recalls they studied the full range of subjects, though not all of them quite held her full attention. Home Economics was her favourite lesson. 'I was not a model pupil. I am afraid I played truant rather a lot. A couple of us used to go off together around Selsey village. We used to hang around the coffee bars.'

The pupils converged on the school from Selsey itself, the Witterings, Sidlesham, Almodington and other neighbouring communities, which meant that the pupils tended to disperse at the end of the day. 'In the evenings we didn't really meet up with each other much, except for those that were in the village with you. There was no transport unless your parents were wealthy enough to have a car.'

For real entertainment, Sheila would head north to Chichester and enjoy the choice of three cinemas – the Gaumont (now a disused swimming pool), the Granada (now McDonalds) and the Odeon (now Iceland).

'Out of preference we tended to go to the Odeon down South Street, just because of what was on there. We'd always go and watch the latest Elvis film. One particular friend and I were Elvis mad. We just thought he was great at the time. ... I look at his films now and wonder what the hell did we find in them!' Sheila remembers that she couldn't afford Elvis' records: 'It was as much as we could do to afford to go to the pictures!'

[3 October 1996]

Alan cherishes Life through a Lens

The photographic skills of Donnington's Alan Bell captured aspects of Chichester High School for Boys in the first half of the 1960s. From the formal sports and form photos to the passport-style photos needed for college, Mr Bell was the man behind the camera.

He was employed to look after the school grounds, but before taking up the job he'd been doing semi-professional photographic work at Worthing – a sideline which soon came in useful at the school.

Mr Bell had worked in horticulture but was out of work in 1959 when he saw an advertisement for the job of school groundsman. He applied and got it. For the next six years he took photos of rugby teams, football teams, cricket teams, staff, classes and prefects – pictures which took longer to set up than they did to take.

Mr Bell was also there to record a rugby match against a team from Chichester's twin city of Chartres in 1961. He also recorded for posterity a 1960s staff versus boys soccer game.

All of it happened under the watchful eye of K.D. Anderson, a headmaster Mr Bell remembers with respect. 'He was known to everyone as KD. He was a man who believed in efficiency, but he was also a very fair man. I got on with him very well. He was a nice chap. ... The boys used to laugh that it was the only school that had a headmaster and a

The staff of Chichester High School for Boys were snapped by Alan Bell in July 1962.

headmistress. His wife was there as well, and she used to be quite a tough character when it came to organising things in the school. She was a teacher and she had quite a lot of say in things.'

One of KD's great characteristics was his fondness for Oxford and Cambridge. 'Whenever one of the pupils had got through, he would get the caretaker or myself to run up the Union Jack on the flag mast.'

For photos for entrance to college, KD was a stickler for appearance. A passport-style photo was required, and many a time Mr Bell would be called on to take it.

'He was very fussy', Mr Bell recalls. If the boy didn't look smart enough, Mr Bell would have to take the photo again.

'On one occasion he had me take this chap three times. He liked to run a good ship.'

Inevitably, Mr Bell saw a great deal of the boys. He got on well with them. 'I had a lot to do with them. I used to maintain all the grounds, both the flowers and the fields, marking out all the pitches and maintaining the posts and balls.' He well remembers the leather balls which got heavy when wet. For the sports photos, he would paint one with the year for a player to hold.

Mr Bell gave up the job when he got 'chesty' one winter, and the chance came up of taking an indoor job with the electricity board.

It was another stage in a varied working life. Mr Bell had started out with a couple of years in a bank in 1945. He later became a photographer covering a number of weddings in the area back in the days when a single photographer could easily control a hundred guests. Remember, these were the days when the official photographer was probably the only one there with a camera. For a while Mr Bell even did his own developing. The 1950s were the days when colour photography was first coming in.

[9 December 1999]

How Terry and Erica went down the Aisle with Miss Davies

Not many pupils end up as their teacher's bridesmaids, but it happened to Terry Franks and Erica Webb. Terry – then Baldwin – and Erica – then Eyles – were pupils at Chichester's Kingsham County Primary School back in the swinging '60s, the teacher was a Miss Davies.

Terry recalls: 'She was talking to another teacher at the time, and Erica and I were walking through the corridor.' As Erica remembers: 'The other teacher remarked that we would make lovely bridesmaids, and that was it really. She asked us to be bridesmaids. We went to Wales for the wedding. That must have been about 1967. I remember we were horrendously sick on the car journey, but my memories are really hazy.'

Erica, born and brought up in Chichester but now living in Littlehampton, recalls that Miss Davies' father was the vicar and took the service. Like Terry, she looks back on her schooldays fondly: 'I was very happy at school. I haven't got any bad memories. On the whole the teachers were very kind. It was quite a strict regime, but I think that was generally the case.'

Terry, who now lives in Sidlesham, agrees: 'It was a good school. It was very friendly and very warm.' She enjoyed the chance to go back there some years later in a different guise.

'I was employed by county for a while, and one of my roles with county was as an education welfare officer. I had responsibilities for a number of schools including Kingsham.

'On visiting the school I came in contact with Mrs Francis who was one of the teachers while I was a pupil there. I attended her retirement do. It was really good to go back into school.'

By then Terry and her family had been to the other side of the world and back.

'I left school to emigrate to Australia with my parents. We returned to this country when I was in my fourth year at secondary school. … I think at the time there was a lot of promotion in terms of going out to Australia. There were assisted passages. I think it was an assisted passage that we went out to New South Wales with. … It was a fantastic experience, but it was incredibly difficult to uproot because of the strong friendships in the school. Not only did I go to school with Erica and a couple of others but we lived in the same road. We spent our school life together and our home life together as well. To uproot like that was very strange. It took some time to settle in Australia.'

Her principal impression was how archaic the country was: 'I remember the school system out there being so different. Instead of preparing myself to go to secondary school, I had to return to primary school out there. … The schoolmasters at the time at this particular school still wore the gown and hat, and a lot of their curriculum centred on the history of Australia. … I found at the time that it was all very very different and in some ways backward. There were all sorts of different cultures in the classroom – aborigines and so on. In my class at Kingsham, as far as I can remember, we were all English. Out there I was in the minority.' But after a while she started to make friends, and the barriers dropped: 'I became acclimatised to their way of life.'

[29 July 1999]

Opposite: *Chichester's South Street is decorated for the Festival of Britain, 1951.*

Class of '69 was the Last

Lavant mums Lisa Ayling and Jane Haskins well remember their last day at Chichester's Central Junior Girls School. The day they left in 1969 was the end of an era. The boys and girls schools were amalgamated and the old girls school in Chapel Street was pulled down.

Lisa and Jane were Barns and Clayton respectively back then. They lost touch but then ended up near neighbours in Heron Close. Now they want to organise a big get-together to mark the 25th anniversary of the passing of the Central Girls School, a school they still remember with affection. Jane recalls: 'They knocked the building down, and it's now a block of flats called Providence Place. There isn't even a plaque to say that the Central Girls School once stood there. ... It would be nice to put something up. If perhaps we got together, we could get the council to do something.'

Looking back, Lisa remembers a school which in many ways was still very much in the Victorian mould. 'We had classroom dividers, and the ceilings were really high. Some of the teachers were getting modern, but there were a couple of teachers that were still very Victorian.'

Another memory is the outside loos. Pupils had to walk across the playground to reach them. 'I remember one year there was thick snow and the teachers had to clear a path to the toilets', Jane says.

'When the end came for the school, people were quite sad to be leaving. I can remember thinking I don't want to leave and that it would be nice if they kept us as a girls school.' The school did have its drawbacks, though. There was no sports field. Sports meant a trip to Priory Park. As for school dinner, this meant a trip to a hut in what is now St Cyriac's car park.

Jane also recalls headmistress Mrs Taylor: 'She was strict but very nice. We used to have a system if you did good work, you got a star. If you got ten stars, on a Friday afternoon you could go and collect a jelly baby.' The fourth-years would take turns to go to the shops for the jelly babies and also to buy a packet of tea for the headmistress.

Lisa recalls Mrs Taylor would play Handel's Water Music. Neither Lisa nor Jane know, though, whether she is still in the area. 'We would like to contact the teachers as well. They seemed really old at the time, but they must have been under 60. ... We'd like to contact as many people as possible. If we find there is no one around or if they are scattered all around the world, then we won't be able to do anything. If we get lots of people, well, we'll see...'

So, come on, then. Who's out there who remembers wearing those navy blue gym slips with green flashes?

[25 August 1994]

Chapter Seven

YOUTH COMES OF AGE

Happy City Childhood Days

Growing up in post-war Chichester brought happy and memorable times for Barry Tester. At the Lancastrian Boys' School he formed friendships which have lasted a lifetime, and at Fratton Park he saw the likes of Sir Stanley Matthews.

A keen footballer then, Mr Tester, now 56, played for Chichester Boys' Club. Come Saturday, there was nothing he liked better than to go to Portsmouth with his dad to see the real thing. 'It was a different atmosphere then,' he recalls. 'There was never any trouble. I used to have a wooden block to stand on, and the children would be passed right down to the front so that they could see.' The community spirit, engendered by war, lived on in the late 1940s and early 1950s.

'There was a very close togetherness with the people generally. I don't think I'd want another war to bring it back, but it did bring people together. ... Everybody used to help everybody else during the war. The fathers were away, and it was all the mothers together with all the children.'

Mr Tester's time with the boys' club was an extension of that wartime era of friendliness. 'It was a way of bringing together young lads eager for a game and a chat. ... We used to play football, and we used to play darts and snooker. It was also a good social thing and a way of keeping us herberts off the streets. It was good fun.'

He also remembers fondly his school days at the Lancastrian – despite the threat of the slipper which hung over offenders. A slap of the slipper or a rap over the knuckles was the price miscreants paid for getting caught looking through the fence at the girls in the school next door. 'That was the worst thing we did. It wasn't ever anything very drastic', he recalls.

'I was very fortunate at school. I always stayed in the top grade. I managed to keep in the A-stream by the skin of my teeth. I suppose that made a difference. I imagine you get on a lot better for that.' Mr Tester remembers the school as a place where educational standards were high, a progressive place where discipline was in place but where the academic and the extra-curricular mixed in just the right proportions.

It was also a place where he was free to pursue his interest in sports. He recalls Mr Pontin and Mr Heather as excellent games teachers, inspirations to the children in their charge. 'There was football and there was cricket. We were all very keen on sports.'

Rationing lived on, but little war damage remained. Chichester had escaped relatively lightly, though memories of the plane crashing onto the steam laundry lived on.

Mr Tester, who then lived in Cambrai Avenue, well remembers the blown-in windows the crash caused.

But as a post-war pupil, such things seemed a long time ago. Stanley Matthews beckoned, the lure of football was strong, and the world was getting back on its feet.

[8 December 1994]

Days of Innocence and Rock 'n' Roll

Today she's a leading district councillor and a respected youth leader. Today he works at Covers, the timber and DIY company. But in the 1950s, they were Chichester's leading dancers. The floor would empty and the crowds would start to gather whenever Anne Scicluna and Brian 'Spyder' Clear started to jive or rock and roll. 'We were the best,' Anne recalls. 'I reckon we could still give them a run for their money.' 'Provided I've taken my heart tablets,' Brian admits.

Friends in a new era ... Anne Scicluna (left), Graham Haigh of Worthing, and Joan Boxall of Petworth in 1959.

It was an exciting era. 'We learnt from watching the films like Rock Around The Clock,' Brian remembers. 'We felt that if they could do it, we could do it. We hadn't ever heard any music like it before. ... You went to a dance and it was waltzes and quick steps, and then this film, The Blackboard Jungle, came out about rebellious schoolchildren. The music was Bill Haley. It just grabbed us. Everyone wanted to do it.'

'We were good, and we knew it,' says Anne. 'The skill was the rhythm. If you didn't have a sense of rhythm, you couldn't do it. Stamina came into it as well, and balance. If you were dancing like fury and you got out of breath, you had so many people watching that you couldn't give in.'

Fashion also played its part. 'Stiletto heels helped. If you are dancing that sort of dance with stiletto heels, and you are kicking your heels up, you tend to get given a bit of space by the others!'

Being able to keep up with the fashions was a factor in other ways too, Anne recalls. Trad jazz came along, and Anne and Brian would dance to trad jazz at the Ritz.

'And then there was another club down at Fishbourne that was for modern jazz. We decided to go down there and we danced. It was a different rhythm to what we were used to. You could either halve it or double it. We started, and everyone formed a big crowd around us. The music went on and on. We ended up exhausted.' Brian moved into singing and still has a band today. But they look back on the '50s as a happy time. 'We enjoyed life,' Anne recalls. 'We had to make our own entertainment. Very few people had televisions.'

Brian also remembers it fondly: 'There was no real latent violence around. There were a few teddy boys that would have a punch-up, but that would just be a few blows and a lot of shouting. And there weren't drugs around. People didn't seem to have alcohol problems. We just drank alcohol. No problem. ... Sex was something that was talked about and sniggered about. If someone got pregnant, they just disappeared for six months. Nobody was supposed to know anything about it. The pressure on females to remain virgins was horrendous.

'I remember a girl tried to perform her own abortion with knitting needles and did herself an awful lot of damage. That was the kind of pressure.'

But Anne reckons that the pressures – different pressures – are generally greater on today's young people. 'We didn't realise we were poor. Looking back, during the war we were probably deprived, but we didn't feel deprived because we didn't know anything else. After the war, in the 1950s, you could suddenly go down the road to the shops to buy sweets. They were exciting times.'

[1 April 1999]

A rock and roller abroad ... Anne Scicluna in 1959.

Home after 40 Years

A London man facing life in a wheelchair has made an emotional return to Chichester after 40 years away. Brian Garner, aged 58, who is suffering a gradual spinal deterioration, came back to the city for two days to revisit the scenes of his youth.

Mr Garner says he could lose the use of his limbs over the next couple of years or in a couple of months time go ahead with an operation which has very limited chances of success. Either way, he reckons, his days of mobility are looking severely limited. Hence his decision to come back briefly to Chichester for the first time in four decades.

'It's absolutely incredible the differences you can see. Shopping is definitely better, I don't like the one-way systems and obviously the Cathedral hasn't changed a bit. ... I was here in the days of Bishop Bell. That was when the jukeboxes were not allowed after 8.30pm on a Saturday night. That was one of the things that stuck in my mind. We used to come out of the Gaumont cinema and go to the 43rd Grill in West Street and the music would just go off at 8.30pm. They would have to switch it off.'

Other changes include the huge increase in the number of tourists on the streets. 'There are far more now, obviously. It was more of a family community in my day here. It was very very close-knit.'

Born in Kent, Mr Garner was evacuated to Bracklesham Bay in 1944 and remained in the Chichester area until 1957, since when he'd never been back. 'Bracklesham Bay when we moved down there was all barbed wire and there were all tank blocks and so on. You really shouldn't have gone down to the beach but we did and we used to find life belts from ships that had sunk.

'I went back there yesterday afternoon and I just couldn't recognise it with all the blocks of flats. Bracklesham Bay has lost everything really. It is just one mass of holiday homes and holiday maisonettes.'

As for Chichester, Mr Garner noticed sadly its lack of cinemas, recalling fondly the days when there were three. 'They were always packed on Saturdays. That was in the days of the teddy boys. I was one too. There were five of us that used to go around together. ... Every cinema used to have its own group of people that used to go. The Granada was known as the flea pit. That was the worst one of the lot. ... The Odeon had a good reputation, and we used to go to the Gaumont. You would know where everyone would be sitting. Everyone had their own seats that they would always go to.'

During his return trip, Mr Garner was hoping to renew contact with a number of friends from long ago, particularly his ex-girlfriend who, he is sure, lives still in the city. She worked in the bindery department of R.J. Acford's printers in the 1950s when Mr Garner was also an employee.

Mr Garner would also love to hear from Ted Garnett who worked in the mono-type casting and was a great buddy of his back then. 'There was also someone who used to look after me called Taffy Thomas. He was in the warehouse department. There was also a lady called Wendy Matthews.' Fond memories of a Chichester which has long since gone.

[16 November 1995]

Liberating Times after Dreary Era

Keith Boxall looks back fondly on the 1960s – a time of liberation after an era of tough struggle. Chichester-born Mr Boxall left the city's Lancastrian School in 1961, just as a new age was dawning. 'It was freedom for teenagers in many respects. We had gone through the 1950s which you can see since were really pretty dull and dreary. For about ten years after the war, it was a struggle to get the economy going. The wages were not so good, and then you get into the '60s and suddenly you had an era where there was more or less full teenage employment.

'There was pocket money for teenagers, and you had the scooter age arriving, the mods and the rockers. You had money to buy the clothes that were fashionable. We had The Beatles breaking out in 1963. I was then nineteen. I was certainly a Beatles fan. They were different, trend-setting, appealing to the opposite sex, and I suppose we tried to emulate them in some ways. We followed the trends.'

Mr Boxall, who now lives near Andover, remembers going to see them in Portsmouth. It was all a long way removed from the era he was born into, a couple of months after D-Day. In fact, because of the war, he wasn't even born in hospital. St Richard's had been taken over for the post D-Day casualties. Mr Boxall was born instead in a private nursing home. He grew up in Cleveland Road and attended Whyke Infants School before going to the Central School, now the New Park Centre.

'It was all boys and it was quite a lively school. We had a good bunch of teachers there. Some of them were pre-war teachers and knew what they were doing. Others had been in the war and some of them thought they were still involved. They were disciplinarians. But it was a good school to go to, within walking distance. The headmaster was Mr Greeves. He seemed to get on well with most people there.'

After that, Mr Boxall went to the Lancastrian School, the secondary modern which shared a site with the high school. 'It was a new school when I went there, and they were trying to create the right impression. They had a full range of curricular activities and quite a good emphasis on sports. All the sports facilities that you wanted were there.

'Academically the staff set out to make their mark against the high school. The high school was part of the same complex but was entirely separate and there was an intense rivalry – especially when it snowed! There were huge snowball fights. ... The academic class that I went into came out of it pretty well. I got what was known at the school as the Barton Testimonial which was an academic award. It was one of these charity things that were set up by a benefactor to the school.

'The headmaster there at the time was a Mr Roy Lewis, and he was firm and fair. He was known as Lewie. We were always in awe of having to go before Lewie for disciplinary reasons. They were a bit more liberal with canes and slippers then than they are now.'

Mr Boxall admits he was occasionally on the wrong end of a bit of punishment – though never for anything too serious. And then, all too soon, school was over and the 1960s were opening up. Looking back, Mr Boxall can't help wondering what became of his classmates ...

[9 September 1999]

Grahame, Tony, Gary ... The Object!

For the first time in more than 30 years Grahame Vick and Tony Russell have just heard their old demo tape. And they don't mind admitting they were impressed. The studio facilities were pretty primitive back then; the sound technology was nothing like it is today; but their demo, featuring their own song, Moonshine, plus a cover of All I Need, captured exactly what The Object were about.

The Object, c.1967.

The Object were one of Chichester's most popular home-grown bands of the mid-1960s, and, by common agreement, they were good. People were so keen to know what they were up to that their practice sessions at *The Hole In The Wall* would attract almost as many people as their gigs.

Grahame, now an officer with West Sussex County Council, recalls that the five-piece first got together in about 1965, playing mainly pop and rock and roll, picking up on the big hits of the day. 'We would do some Beatles and Rolling Stones and Small Faces stuff.'

Some of the practices would be in the living room at Tony's parents' house. Even the neighbours didn't mind – too much. 'The neighbours used to turn their TVs down to listen to us, probably because they couldn't hear their TVs anyway. They used to say "Ooh, we liked that one you were doing last night." They never ever moaned.'

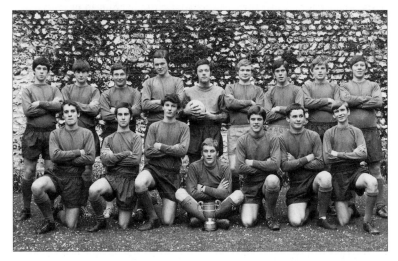

Grahame and friends in the Chichester Boys' Club football team, c.1965.

The living room was for the sessions where they ground out the basics. Larger halls were used for the sessions where they added the amplification. Grahame was the bass guitarist – not a particularly good one, he insists, but bass guitarist all the same. Tony, now a landscape gardener, alternated rhythm and lead guitar and also did some of the lead and some of the backing vocals. The other members of the band were Tim Green, believed now to be a music publisher in Germany; Gary Beacher, apparently still in the area; and Clive Clayton, the drummer and apparently now on the Isle of Wight.

Tony well remembers singing The Beatles' Michelle, but one of their most popular numbers was The Small Faces' All Or Nothing. Gary sounded so much like Steve Marriott that they would often have to sing the song four times in an evening. 'We tried to keep up with all the number ones,' Tony remembers. 'If it was The Beatles at number one or The Rolling Stones at number one, or whoever, we would try to do the song. ... We used to have one of these very old-fashioned tape recorders with a spool. Top Of The Pops was on Thursday and we would push the mike up against it and tape the lot. We'd write down the words and try to get the music.'

Grahame Vick, c.1966.

Locally, they built up a strong following. They were 15 and 16, they were local and they were a novelty. But after a couple of years they went their separate ways, and the band folded. None of them thought too much more about it until they were drafted in to provide their memories for Chichester District Museum's popular Teen Spirit exhibition – an experience which brought them a particularly pleasant blast from their past.

The band had made a demo tape back in their heyday, but there were only ever about a dozen copies in existence, and Tony and Grahame hadn't kept one. But the museum's research for the exhibition unearthed a copy and, for the first time in more than 30 years, Tony and Grahame had the chance to hear The Object.

They were both pleasantly surprised.

'It's got a good live sound,' Tony reckons. 'It's what we sounded like.' Their excitement, however, isn't such that the band is about to reform. Tony and Grahame reckon they'd be able to hammer out a few songs after just a few hours together, but the cost in equipment would be high and they are vague about where the other members are the band are now.

So it looks likely that The Object will remain a memory for the moment …

[11 March 1999]

If you're going to Tangmere Airfield …

The '60s were the decade when British pop music led the world. Andy Ifould was among the millions to enjoy a wonderful time. Andy, now an environmental standards officer for Chichester District Council, reckons the swinging '60s certainly swung in Chichester.

Andy was growing into adulthood at a time when Status Quo would turn up at Butlin's in Bognor – a time when Tangmere airfield, far from being a home to a museum, was a thriving venue capable of attracting the likes of Jimmy James and The Vagabonds. Tangmere – though Andy admits he wasn't there to see them – also hosted gigs by The Move and The Tremeloes.

It was a time, Andy recalls, when the barriers were starting to break down. 'You were starting to get rock concerts on the Isle of Wight. I suppose it all spun off from the flower power of the era when everybody seemed to be more relaxed about life. … Attitudes certainly seemed to be getting easier. Whether perhaps it was the philosophy of "let life go past" or not, I don't know. There was a lot of "step off the treadmill of life for a while and then get back on". … It's difficult to compare when you have nothing to compare it with, but I would far rather have been young then than now. There is more violence out there now, more vandalism. Vandalism in those days didn't seem to be anywhere near what it is now.'

And there was most definitely a buzz about the social life back then. 'I was living in Lavant, but you spent a lot of your social time in Chichester because that's where it was all happening. You used to go to places like the Boys Club, St George's Hall, Whyke, the youth wing at the Lancastrian School. And they would have groups at Tangmere at the airbase. They seemed to have the better groups. There was more money at an airbase.'

Butlin's in Bognor was also a venue. It was there that he first saw Status Quo, an experience which has made him an appreciator – he hesitates to say fan – ever since.

These were easy days: 'We had our own teenage anguishes, I suppose, but when you reflect now, it was just nothing. Everybody, I think, was concerned about their image, as they are today. But it wasn't so high-profile back then. Everybody wanted to look the part with the costume of the time. If you rode a scooter, you used to wear a Parka. But it wasn't so pressurised as it is now.'

Landlords were certainly laid-back. Andy would think nothing of getting served in a pub at the tender age of 15. He recalls that things were less formal back then.

'You could drive around the four streets of Chichester. If you saw someone you knew you would pull up in front of the Cathedral and have a jaw for ten minutes. Or you would park up and meet people around Chichester.

'The two main coffee bars were the El Bolero in South Street and one called Sergio's in St Martin's Street. There was a certain undercurrent of rivalry between the two groups that would use them.' Drugs were on the scene generally, but Andy wasn't interested, and they certainly weren't so prevalent. 'I had no interest in drugs. If I couldn't get a good time with a couple of beers, then I was wasting my time!'

The opposite sex was a feature which loomed large – larger, oddly, than he reckons it does today. 'It was part of the courtship game of life – though that's perhaps not the best terminology. I have got boys now and their interest in girls seemed to start later than ours did back then. I can remember that at 14 and 15 we were hanging around the girls ... '

[4 March 1999]

A young Andy Ifould, a child of the 1960s and proud of it! Pictured in 1968.

The Day a Rolling Stone dropped in for Tea

Not many people can claim among their memories the day hell-raiser Rolling Stones guitarist Keith Richards dropped in for tea. But these, it seems, were the circles in which the now legendary Barnham Boys moved in the late '60s and early '70s. These were the days of hippy-dom – days of cotton loon trousers, kaftans and afghan coats.

Chichester-based writer Bryan Gartside, who writes under the name Bryan Roy, was one of the younger members of the Barnham Boys. A key figure among the Barnham Boys was Peter Jones, and it was at his house that Keith Richards dropped in one Sunday afternoon in 1971. 'He hung around for the afternoon and had tea with us,' Bryan recalls. 'He was with Anita Pallenberg. They were fairly quiet. They certainly weren't being pretentious or flashy, but as youngsters we were pretty much in awe of this guy. ... I used to like the Stones. They weren't my favourites, but Keith Richards lived down at Wittering. Some of the guys had been down there and, I suppose, he was on a return visit.

'They were very friendly and sociable. Pop stars these days tend to be more reclusive and defensive because there are so many people who might want to take a shot at them like they shot John Lennon or mob them or whatever. But back in 1971 there wasn't such a paranoia. Things were like that in those days. Things just happened spontaneously.'

Bryan Gartside with his grandmother in Barnham in August 1970, just before he left for the Isle of Wight pop festival.

The Barnham Boys were avid adherents of hippy philosophy and culture, and that meant plenty of scrapes and escapades. Bonnie and Clyde styles came and went with their sinister gangster suits. Flared trousers were in, and Easy Rider chopper bikes were on the way. Blue Beat, ska and mods were part of life. And so was the El Bolero coffee bar in Chichester's South Street, pre-1970. Another significant venue was the Rex ballroom in Bognor, the site on which The Watershed now stands.

'People don't really appreciate and realise that the council destroyed the best two venues in Bognor – the Rex ballroom and the Esplanade theatre. The Rex ballroom was a significant landmark on the seafront.

'At the Rex I saw people like Status Quo, Black Sabbath, Marc Bolan and Hawkwind. There was a whole range of popular groups there, and it was the most magnificent building. It had an open-plan dance floor and for the young people it was the most fantastic place to go.'

It's one of the places which doubtless will be evoked in Bryan's next novel. Following a group of adolescents around the Barnham area, it will even take the name Barnham Boys. And in the meantime Bryan is keen to promote a Barnham Boys reunion.

[29 October 1998]

Life-Changing Moment leads to Life in the Theatre

It was Julian Sluggett's road to Damascus, he recalls. The light was blinding; it lasted a week; and it has shaped his life.

Theatre director Julian, who lives at Southbourne, has gone on to produce shows both locally and nationally. He probably wouldn't have done if he hadn't had a life-changing stay at Lodge Hill, the educational residential centre near Pulborough.

The centre was nearly lost a few years ago when the county council decided to sell it off and plough the cash elsewhere. But the decision provoked furore, and a trust emerged which raised the money to buy the centre and run it independently.

Julian Sluggett and friends enjoy a life-changing stay at Lodge Hill.

The trust enjoyed huge support across the county. Countless thousands of people rallied to the cause, spurred on by memories such as those which Julian still cherishes.

Julian enjoyed a residential drama summer school at Lodge Hill in 1960. It decided the way his life was going to go. He got involved through friends of his: 'I was at a loss to know what to do during the summer really. It turned out to be almost a coming of age thing. They said to me "hey, look, there is a spare place on this drama course." ... I had always been interested in the theatre. My parents used to take me to the Old Theatre Royal in Portsmouth. I actually saw the farewell tour of Laurel and Hardy. I would have been about ten.'

Sadly, he doesn't have great memories of it: 'They did the old bar-bershop routine, but it was so slow. It was tired. There wasn't much sparkle.' The chorus girls made up for it, though ...

Julian thinks he may also have seen Charlie Chaplin at the venue: 'They used to have different variety acts coming in each week. It was the touring variety shows. They would call in at Portsmouth, do a week and then go somewhere else. There wasn't much by way of drama there. That was at the Kings in Southsea, and I would go there too.

'That was my first introduction into it. I suppose I had always had this thing about drama in my life, but it was Lodge Hill that really did it for me. That was the turning point. It was like being on the road to Damascus – the blinding light ... ' Julian was just 15, and there was a magic about the whole thing: 'It was a wonderful week. It was just a magical gathering, and it was very intensive stuff.'

Julian has kept the programme. It shows there wasn't a moment to spare. Scripts, speech training, rehearsals, movement sessions and the like came thick and fast.

WEST SUSSEX COUNTY COUNCIL·
Service of Youth

D R A M A
S U M M E R
S C H O O L

LODGE HILL
RESIDENTIAL CENTRE
30th July - 7th August 1960

C.W.W. ⟨⟩AD, B·Sc., Ph.D.
Director of Education

The programme becomes a souvenir for the students on the 1960 drama summer school at Lodge Hill.

There was even a talk from CFT founder Leslie Evershed-Martin on the proposed Chichester Festival Theatre.

'We got from the summer school the whole construction process of plays, how a narrative works, how to make narrative links, really getting to the quintessence of the characters in a play. These guys that were teaching us were really amazingly dedicated. Every split second was used. There was not a moment when we were not working or discussing or working up new ideas. It was about stage management, costumes, costume design, make-up, everything ... '

And Lodge Hill's isolated location up a hill was a great spur to concentration, Julian recalls: 'We were just totally immersed in what we were doing ... '

It certainly inspired Julian to become involved in the very early days of the Festival Theatre. He worked there for the first four seasons, starting off as a dish-washer.

'It was an incredible time ... manic. There used to be so much dish-washing and because I lived just around the corner I was given the keys to go in and help get things ready. The telephone was constantly going.'

Julian ended up doing theatre tours, and on one such tour, he recalls, he had a very august guest – none other than the CFT's first artistic director, Laurence Olivier.

[6 December 2001]

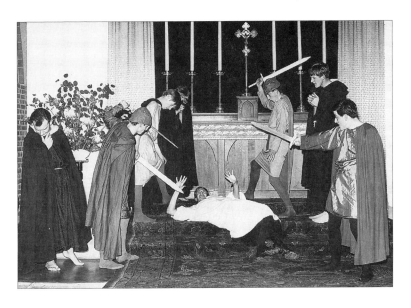

Julian stars as Becket in a 1962 youth production of Murder in the Cathedral *in St George's Church, Whyke, Chichester.*

Justice at last for the Nearly Man ...

A Chichester landlady reckons the new wave of Beatlemania will at last do justice to her uncle – the man The Beatles spurned. Angie Parsons says Pete Best's depression was long and damaging after he was thrown out of the band by Beatles manager Brian Epstein. Best was discarded in favour of Ringo Starr in a move which brought the rejected drummer to the brink of suicide.

Angela and Nick Parsons celebrate Angela's Beatles links at the Eastgate *pub, Chichester.*

'Now with the new Beatles album coming out, my uncle might at last get some of the recognition that he deserves,' Angie says. It's a recognition which Angie is already fostering at *The Eastgate* pub where she has put up a signed photo of Uncle Pete in full flow during his brief Beatles days. Some of the tracks Pete Best recorded with The Beatles are on the newly-released Beatles Anthology 1.

The royalties from them will give Best a little inkling of what he might have ended up earning if The Beatles hadn't kicked him out. Some sources say he stands to earn £7 million or more from the project, but Angie reckons it will probably be significantly less. Even so, it will still be considerable.

'But he deserves it. I get the feeling that it is going to happen for him now after all these years.' Best is currently touring in Japan, and Angie reckons his future with his new band is bound to be helped by the huge reawakening of Fab Four-mania.

All the same, the fact that she was so nearly related to one quarter of a pop revolution is something Angie takes in her stride.

'We sort of took it for granted. To me he was just my uncle. I never really thought of him as a celebrity. It was just very hard what happened to him and it wasn't really something we talked about.'

Angie, aged 32, says: 'He was very depressed about it all at the time. Everyone says I am like his wife personality-wise. She just gets on with her life. That's the way she is. Because of her strength and normality she pulled Pete through.'

Now Best is publicly reconciled with his past, ready to put the swinging (and stinging) '60s behind him. And he is even being quoted as saying that a reunion with Paul McCartney, George Harrison and Ringo Starr is just a matter of time.

Angie however, doesn't, rate the chances terribly high of it happening in Chichester. She hasn't seen her uncle for a year and probably won't see him again until a family wedding next year.

But in the meantime Pete will peer down from the poster on the wall at The Eastgate and Angie will continue to play in the pub the '60s music she loves. 'I am very proud of him and what he has done', she says.

[30 November 1995]

Chapter Eight

ENTERTAINMENT

Fame beckoned as an Ovaltiney

Everyone knows the little ditty 'We are the Ovaltineys'. Few people can claim to have been one.

Vic Valente, who lives at Fittleworth, was one of the original members of the Ovaltineys Concert Party and toured the country with his fellow Ovaltineys in the 1930s.

Vic was born in Midhurst in 1921 and his stage career started not many years later. His wasn't a theatrical family, but the theatre was in his blood somewhere, and out it came.

'Dad and I used to go up to London for music lessons, and when I was about nine I was considered proficient enough to become involved in a show in Portsmouth.'

Vic was a juvenile accordion player in a band run by a Madame Courtenay who became his tutor in Portsmouth.

'Our first show was at the Coliseum and I think I recall that talent scouts were there. Apparently there were some in the audience, and from there we did another theatre in Portsmouth, the Theatre Royal. We also did the Kings in Southsea … It was very exciting. I was able to put up with a family in Portsmouth for a year. Whilst I was there I was being taught the rudiments of the theatre, how to walk on stage and so on – the kinds of things that I don't think are taught nowadays. I was big-headed enough to think that I knew everything there was as a nine, ten, eleven-year-old. We then did a show called Our Kiddies. I have a feeling we went back to the Coliseum and did the show.'

A tour of London and the provinces followed, and then the show was transformed into the Ovaltineys Concert Party, an advertising show for the popular drink. 'I was one of the originals. I used to play the accordion in those days. It was broadcast from Radio Luxembourg every Sunday morning, the only commercial radio programme at the time. We all said that we were broadcast from Luxembourg, but it was recorded in London.

'Then we did this long tour throughout England. I think I must have performed at most of the theatres in the UK. We went to theatres throughout the British Isles. … Then we came back on the London circuit. I was very proud and honoured that we played the London Palladium two or three times. To do that at that age was really quite something.

'This went on for some years and then unfortunately there was a family break-up and mum took off with another bloke. That fouled the whole family up. ... Unfortunately it was felt better that I left the stage while my father was in the situation he was in. He was taken to hospital because of what they called nerves in those days. I seem to recall him being in hospital for some time after mother left him. ... So I came back to Midhurst. After some time and after various jobs I became an errand boy. It was quite embarrassing coming back like that after being the "local boy made good". It wasn't easy.

'Then somebody suggested why didn't I give music lessons. I started doing that around the place and started getting a few people together. Somebody then suggested why didn't I form a dance band. After a while I thought that that was a good idea, but not just accordions.

'There were other instrumentalists in the area. I advertised in the *Midhurst Times* as it was in those days, and I got quite a selection. I formed a ten-piece swing band and we did extremely well. We took over the area, more or less.'

Vic Valente And His Rhythm Boys are still fondly remembered around Midhurst, but sadly the war intervened. The Second World War took Vic to North Africa, Sicily and Italy where he was wounded and eventually sent home.

Things were not the same, though, after the war. The band members had gone their separate ways and it just wasn't possible for the Rhythm Boys to get back together again.

But Vic's life continued its unpredictable way. 1965 saw him emigrate to Australia where for ten years he travelled the outback towing a caravan and doing up sheep and cattle stations, mostly from knowledge gained in a library. Whilst in Australia he also worked on radio, producing and presenting his own programmes and also serving as a news presenter. After 30 years in the Antipodes he decided it was time to come home. Vic now lives in Fittleworth with his wife Jean and his memories of his days as an Ovaltiney.

[5 September 1996]

Joan: a Friend to the Young Picture-Goers

Joan Cooper is Aunty Joan to hundreds of men and women throughout Chichester. Nearly 50 years on, Joan is still remembered fondly by the countless children she ushered through Chichester's old Gaumont cinema.

Joan, who has since worked for Gunning's betting shop for more than 30 years, joined the Gaumont in Eastgate Square (now the disused swimming pool) in 1942 as a 17-year-old usherette and left as manageress when the cinema closed in 1960.

Looking back, she recalls an exciting era when the cinema was a major focus for the city's life – not just for the adults who flocked to the cinema every evening, but for the children who came 'along on Saturday mornings greeting everybody with a smile'. Even now, Joan can still recite the seat prices. She's certainly got a store of tales to tell about her cinema days.

'In the town of Chichester there was nothing, and going to the cinema was a treat. People used to love to see the Gaumont news and know what was going on in the war.

The cinema was a key part of Chichester life during the Second World War, through the 1950s and into the 1960s. And Cicestrians were never short of choice ...

The old ladies would come in the afternoons, and it was more like a social gathering than pictures are today. ... 'If there was going to be some fish at Kimbell's, which was a big fish shop, or some fruit, if there was an inkling of that going around, they would come to the pictures and then queue up after that.'

As for the films themselves, Joan confesses she was never a big fan: first priority was getting the people in and comfortable, rather than watching the picture.

Another important task was to promote the films. Grass skirts, cowboy kits and even wedding dresses were all part of a day's work in Joan's 18 years at the Gaumont.

But some of the favourite memories come from the Saturday mornings when she was Aunty Joan to everyone. ... 'We used to get the children in and give them talks about growing up, how to treat people and how to get the best out of life, how to be helpful. ... You used to give them projects like how to make things such as fancy hats or books with cuttings or collecting things.'

And then after the lecture, the Gaumont Cinema Club would launch into its film, with Shirley Temple and Tarzan among the favourites. Mickey Mouse and Donald Duck were always popular, and The Lady And The Tramp and Bambi were guaranteed to enchant the children. 'It's lovely to be remembering now', Joan says.

[26 August 1993]

Days of Long Queues and Sticky Pennies!

Hours of standing and handfuls of sticky pennies are what Dorothy Prichard remembers most about her years as cashier at the Gaumont. Now 88, Dorothy, of St Paul's Road, looks back fondly on the busy days Saturday cinema used to bring. 'Saturday was murder what with the children's programme and getting there for opening time. Saturday was a long day, but I liked it.' She never used to get to sit down as she dished out the tickets, and she still feels the effects nearly half a century later.

More unusual and certainly shorter lived were the shingles she apparently caught from touching all the sticky pennies brought in by eager children, at least one of whom, it seems, had chicken pox ... 'That's what they put it down to, though I don't quite see the connection', she admits.

The long queues stretching back are a rather happier memory of her time at the Gaumont. She worked there from 1948 till its closure. And still fresh in her memory is the 'to-do from the clergy' when the Gaumont decided to start opening on Good Fridays.

But despite countless hours at the cinema, Dorothy admits she was no film buff: 'I always used to go in and get some idea about what the film was about so I could answer the people who phoned up wanting to know.' But she didn't extend her knowledge much beyond that.

[26 August 1993]

On the Look-Out for Faint Cinema Fans

It fell to Malcolm Campbell to watch out for the faint and the overwhelmed. He well remembers his duty at Chichester's Granada cinema when the now legendary *Bonnie and Clyde* was first screened. Its violence probably wouldn't create too much of a stir these days but, more than 30 years ago, it had cinema-goers collapsing in the aisles. 'I was on duty in the foyer and had to be on the look-out for patrons who came out of the cinema feeling faint at the end of the performance,' Malcolm recalls.

The cinema building has long since become McDonald's, but for Malcolm the memories linger on. The screening of *The Good, the Bad and the Ugly* was a momentous event; so too was the arrival in Chichester of Richard Attenborough's *Oh What a Lovely War*, with its memorable closing sequence panning out over a field of crosses set up on Brighton racecourse.

'One film Granada was particularly proud of was *Up the Junction* starring Dennis Waterman and Suzy Kendall, the world premiere of which was screened at the Granada Clapham Junction, the film having been set in that part of south London.

Malcolm Campbell in the cinema's publicity room, c.1968.

GRANADA
CHICHESTER
phone 82407

ABHE Production from
The National Theatre of Great Britain

LAURENCE
OLIVIER
AS
OTHELLO
Ⓤ

ALSO STARRING

MAGGIE SMITH

JOYCE REDMAN and

FRANK FINLAY

PRODUCED BY ANTHONY HAVELOCK-ALLAN and JOHN BRABOURNE   DIRECTED BY STUART BURGE

BASED ON JOHN DEXTER'S STAGE PRODUCTION

A BHE PRESENTATION RELEASED THROUGH EAGLE FILMS LTD   TECHNICOLOR · PANAVISION

SPECIAL FILM PRESENTATION
Thursday February 12 For One Day only
at 2.15 & 7.30

Circle Seats 9/-   child 5/-
Stalls Seats 7/-   child 3/-
O.A.P's   3/-   Matinee Only
School parties 2/- per head
Circle Seats Bookable Evening Show

GRANADA   CHICHESTER   82407
SUNDAY FEBRUARY 8 FOR 6 DAYS
(excluding Thursday)

"THE KILLING OF SISTER GEORGE"
COLOR   'X' (LOCAL)

PROGRAMS
SUNDAY   6.30
WEEKDAYS   7.5
SATURDAYS   1.45   4.40   7.45
MATINEE SHOW WEDNESDAY ONLY AT 2.5

A Chichester showing of Laurence Olivier's 1965 film, Othello.

The Killing of Sister George – *A big hit in Chichester in 1969.*

'We had a large board on display in the foyer in Chichester showing the stars arriving for the premiere.'

Looking back, Malcolm recalls that Saturday was generally the most important day to Granada in Chichester. 'In the morning we had the Grenadiers show – the Saturday morning children's club show with special films that were produced by the CFF, the Children's Film Foundation, which is no longer in existence.

'There were serials and general interest films made specifically for children. The most popular item was the Flash Gordon science fiction serial which was in effect the main feature. ... 'The first programme would involve one or two Warner Brothers cartoons and during the interval there were competitions for children and birthday gifts for the members. At Christmas the club's members were invited to a special free show. But these shows in almost all cinemas came to an end with the advent of Saturday morning children's television. I am thinking particularly of the Multi-Coloured Swapshop. And really the admission that was charged didn't keep these shows viable.'

Back in those days the changeover for films was on Sundays. On Saturday evenings the projectionist had to break down the film and prepare it for transit. The film was collected in large metal cases in the dead of night. 'At the time, in the late 1960s, the following week's programme would also be delivered for the Pavilion cinema in Selsey.

Cinema janitor and handyman Harry Johnson in the late 1960s.

The proprietor would come up to collect his programme. The cinema there was very much a village hall-type operation.'

Part also of the change-over was changing the publicity. 'These were the days when there were large frames containing stills and coloured scenes from the week's programme. These were superseded by rather less interesting, internally-illuminated frames.'

Occasionally, for publicity purposes, the cinema would link up with other businesses in the town. 'I can remember taking posters up to the Seafare fish restaurant in Northgate. That was very popular, and I would always bring back fish and chips for the staff's supper in a drinks box covered with a tea towel. That was something of a Saturday evening ritual.

'Some of the staff would seek their liquid refreshment from *The Fleece* pub. I well remember a now deceased relief manager whose opening gambit was always "Salter's here, never fear, where's my beer!"'

The cinema's clientele – as well as staff – was good news for a number of pubs generally. The longest queues the cinema managed were a little before Malcolm's time, with the screening of Cliff Richard's *Summer Holiday*.

'But the most popular films of the late '60s were Walt Disney's *Jungle Book* which seemed to attract almost as many adults as children and enjoyed full houses for three weeks, and *Ring of Bright Water*, based on the Gavin Maxwell novel. It broke the cinema's attendance record.

'Occasionally we would do publicity stunts. One I particularly remember was for Walt Disney's *Love Bug* when a fleet of Volkswagen Beetles with gigantic sunglasses draped over their windscreens formed a cavalcade. On one occasion the cinema was used to recruit film extras for a film called *All the Right Noises* shot at Fontwell racecourse.'

During his time Malcolm got to meet a number of stars from Chichester Festival Theatre, most notably Peter Ustinov. 'He came to the Granada one week-day morning for a special screening of his latest film, Hot Millions. The staff at the Festival Theatre could show their Equity cards and were given free admission to the cinema. There was some resentment that we were not given the same facilities at the theatre. But our staff passes could come in handy if we found ourselves in any town where there was a Granada cinema. If we introduced ourselves, we were treated like VIPs.'

[5 August 1999]

Where there's Brass, there's Music
– as Horn Player Eric will tell you

Eric Tadd has been playing tenor horn for Chichester City Band for 71 years. But he's still five years short of the remarkable record set by his father who joined the band just a couple of months after it started. It's all just part of the strong family feel which has always characterised the band.

Just a couple of years away from its centenary, the band has always thrived on pairs of brothers and on sons and fathers.

Looking at a 1927 picture of the band, Mr Tadd can name every member, tell you their career details, and how they ended up. Two Greens, two Tadds, three Boxalls, two Schmidts ... Mr Tadd, now 83, happily reels off where they worked, who they worked for, and what they achieved.

Those early days were the highlights as far as Mr Tadd is concerned. He received diplomas from 1926-29 as rewards for attendance at around 400 functions and 90 parties, including Christmas carol playing.

He remembers too the band's founder, Robert Bottrill, an impressive-looking man with an impressive moustache, white gloves and a baton. Mr Bottrill started the band in the early part of 1898. A local coal merchant, he was also a first-class trombonist and a man of vision. During a council meeting in June 1897 it was suggested that Chichester should have a band of its own to attend large functions in and around the city.

Eric Tadd, who joined Chichester City Band at 12 and played for 75 years, falling one year short of equalling his father's record.

Chichester City Band by the war memorial in the 1960s, under the baton of Bob Ayling.

The idea caught on and Mr Bottrill took the lead. In 1905 it was registered in Southampton as the Chichester City Brass Band. Later reed and woodwind were added, but it reverted to brass only in the l920s.

Mr Tadd recalls that Mr Bottrill lived in a large three-storey house with front-facing flint walls in Southgate (knocked down for the Avenue de Chartres to be built). But by the time Mr Tadd joined the band in 1923, Mr Bottrill was moving on, having been offered the paid post as resident musical director of the Bognor Town Band on condition of not being MD of both.

By then, Mr Tadd was already four years into what was to become 61 successive brass band championships. The best of these were held at Crystal Palace before it burnt down in 1936. Mr Tadd remembers it as a tremendous structure, basically glass and beautiful inside. Equally memorable were the trips to London to reach it – trips made in charabancs belonging to Lewis and Co, the furniture people. 'They had roll-top hoods and each person was issued with a blanket. It used to be very cold. We used to get going at about six in the morning and sometimes we wouldn't get back until three the morning after.

'It doesn't seem possible but sometimes we would get lost. Sometimes we would be driving around. One time the driver ended up at the gates of some cemetery somewhere, so he had to drive out and try again! It's amazing to think of it now.'

[24 November 1994]

Edward Tadd, a founder member of Chichester City Band. Edward joined at 16 and played for 76 years.

Longevity is the Spice of Life

Funtington Players stalwart John D'Este Eastes has delved deep into the archives to research and write a history of the company. The company celebrated its 25th birthday last year but in its first guise it goes back to the late 1940s.

John explains: 'It has really got two phases. It went from 1949 to the mid-1960s and then it started again in 1970 to the present day. I first joined the Funtington Players in 1966, but the group was in abeyance for a while when the WI hall in West Ashling was declared unsafe. ... For a while we kept going doing nativity and passion plays in the church until we could get going properly again, so really it has been continuous in a way.'

The idea of writing their history started as a request from the company's publicity officer. John seemed the person best placed to tackle the task, but it was far from plain sailing. 'There was a scrapbook which was in the custody of a previous secretary. I also got two old minute books and they took us back to 1953. Then quite recently the original minute book of 1949 came into my hands, having been in the custody of a previous

WOMEN'S INSTITUTE HALL
WEST ASHLING.

THE FUNTINGTON PLAYERS

present

Quiet Week-end

by Esther McCracken

on

THURSDAY, 12th DECEMBER

FRIDAY, 13th DECEMBER,

at 7.30 p.m.

TICKETS : 3/6; 2/6 and 1/6
(Reserved and Numbered)   (Unreserved)

**ALL PROFIT FROM THE PERFORMANCES
WILL BE GIVEN TO U.N.I.C.E.F.**

*Publicity poster for the
Funtington Players'
1957 production of*
Quiet Week-end.

secretary of the society. ... So then it was a question of going through these documents and trying to piece together what happened.'

What emerged was a story which started just four years after the war when a group of people with an interest in entertainment gathered together, largely under the sponsorship of Enid and Norman Dunlop, vicar and vicar's wife.

'I have got a record of a concert that was given in February 1945 by the scouts and youth fellowship in the village and then there are various scrappy reports of pantos being done in the 1945, '46, '47 period. ... Then in 1949 the Funtington Players name occurs for the first time. It looks as though it was started up then as a serious amateur dramatic group. The first production was a play called *Wasn't It Odd* by Kenneth Horne.'

The company continued with a variety of plays until about 1953 when a drop in interest occasioned an extraordinary general meeting with a view to winding the company up.

But the actors pulled back from the brink and the company struggled on doing a major production a year. More problems ensued in the 1960s, but with the 1970 rebirth things finally moved towards the healthy footing the company now enjoys.

Among the 1970s productions John looks back on most fondly is *This Happy Breed*.

'It was probably the most challenging play that we had done up until that time. It is a play which spans 20 years and the cast have got to age across that.'

A scene from For Better
or Worse, *1958. From
left to right, Jeannette
Boys, Edward Halford,
James Lewis and
Geoffrey Plant.*

101

The Funtington Players stage G.R. Myers' The Miracle in 1965 in aid of the Sussex Church Campaign. The picture shows Gamul, the lame man, played by Eric Blogg, being helped by Simon Peter (Ronald Croucher).

Among the recent highlights is *Bequest to the Nation*, a couple of years ago. 'It was a large-cast costume play and it is a play which is very rarely done and yet very topical with the story of Nelson and Lady Hamilton.' As for now, John reckons things couldn't be better: 'I think it must be one of the most 'professional' amateur companies in the area. It has now got a terrific input from theatre people and actors from a much wider area.'

[11 January 1996]

It's the WOADS without end

Sharing ... that's the secret behind a quarter of a century of success for Walberton Operatic and Amateur Dramatic Society (WOADS). This year sees the company celebrate its silver jubilee, and chairman Madeline Doman is delighted to take it right back to where it started. Then named Walberton Choral Group, they first hit the stage in November 1977, back in the days when tickets were a princely 50p a go.

The debut production was Gilbert & Sullivan's *Trial by Jury* – a show they will be reviving for their anniversary year. The second half of the show each night will be a 25th anniversary gala concert – a major retrospective for a busy company.

The concert will be made up of snippets from every musical production they have done over the past 25 years.

Celebrations will continue on the Saturday with a private party – a champagne reception for members and helpers, past and present. Party pieces will be trotted out and the company will enjoy an anniversary dinner. And as ever, the emphasis will be firmly on teamwork. WOADS is a company which doesn't believe in stars and prima donnas.

Madeline's policy is one of rotation. It's a company which gives everyone the chance to shine – and that, believes Madeline, has been a big part of its success.

Madeline Doman and Charles Dixon in Trial by Jury, *1977.*

WOADS stage The Mikado, *1984.*

That and the fact that it's local through and through. Company founder, the late Eve Dods, was a firm believer in keeping things local – a tradition Madeline has been happy to continue.

Strange to think that it was all intended as a one-off … Eve's original intention was to stage a theatrical event to mark the Queen's silver jubilee. Now 25 years later, the Queen's golden jubilee and WOAD's silver jubilee coincide with both going strong.

The company's first *Trial by Jury* was staged in Slindon, one half of a double bill which also included a play, also produced by Eve. World Without Men was performed by the Walberton WI. But everyone enjoyed Trial By Jury so much that they decided to continue. The following year – 1978 – saw the first full-length G&S from the fledgling company, HMS Pinafore. Eve continued to do G&S until 1984 when she decided to retire from production. The society remained active with concerts and workshops until 1989 when Madeline took over producing for the renamed WOS, now based in the new Walberton Village Hall. A new phase had now begun. Drama was now introduced, and Jan Bryan agreed to direct a play. Hence the 1989 double bill – *Trial by Jury* and *Playgoers*.

Madeline continued to direct the musical each year and Jan directed some nine plays for the group until stepping down five years ago when David Fido took over the drama. Since then, he's directed four plays for

WOADS. It all adds up to a wide repertoire with a loyal core membership. Amongst the numbers are plenty of couples, and these in turn often provide the children when required. Beyond the G&S, the company has enjoyed successes with shows including *My Fair Lady*, *The Merry Widow*, *Fiddler on the Roof*, *Pickwick* and *Oliver*! Now, to make sure the flame gets carried forward, Madeline is hoping to celebrate this year's anniversary by starting up a junior section – all part of WOAD's continuity. Founder member and founder treasurer Arthur Spencer is now 80 years plus and still on stage. Peter and Liz Brown, both founder members, are still active, as are Sheila Shepperd and Mike Gammon who were teachers at Walberton School. Charles and Brenda Dixon and Jim Fielder are also founder members who remain involved.

As Madeline says, there are a number of members who could have made it professionally had they chosen to do so. Instead they get their kicks from a happy amateur brigade which sets its standards high and enjoys a flourishing social life grafted on to the on-stage antics.

The policy remains two productions a year, though the musical now moves from February to October, and the play which has traditionally been in the summer now moves to February.

Also coming up in this anniversary year are two murder-mystery events in the summer, plus a staging of *Me and my Girl*, a musical Madeline is delighted to have secured. 'It's not one that's terribly easy to get, especially if you are in a small group,' she said. But it looks likely to be the perfect way to see WOADS into its next quarter century.

[17 January 2002]

The Lost Art of Laughter in the Roar

Reminiscences of a West Sussex exponent of the long lost art of variety are offered in a fascinating new book. Joe O'Gorman, who lived at various places in the county including Barnham and Slindon between 1934 and 1963, was half of a double act with his brother Dave which enjoyed wide popularity in the 1920s, 1930s and 1940s. With their cross-talking crazy comedy they enjoyed a notable success in America in 1932.

Joe's son, Brian, who now lives in Weybridge, recaptures the excitements of their career in *Laughter in the Roar: Reminiscences of Variety and Pantomime* (The Badger Press, Westbury, Wiltshire). 'It's a gathering together of reminiscences of my father who was a variety artist comedian for 50 years. I have joined that up with what I remember of the other people that he worked with and what he told me about it.

'He was a very good raconteur. He didn't put himself out for publicity, but when you got him talking he was fascinating.'

With his brother, Joe started out, like many others, as a dance act: 'Gradually the comedy side developed – crazy comedy. They became very well known. They were always working.'

Some of the work still survives: 'They made records. I have copies of those on tape. I have also got three short films of them. One of them is good because they are working with an audience.'

Born in 1890, Joe died in 1974. He spent much of his life in West Sussex, an escape, he said, from the Northern industrial towns. He liked the sunshine and fresh air.

Mr O'Gorman reckons his comedy stands the test of time: 'I find them extremely amusing.

'I remember them from my earliest days when I was watching from the side of the stage. Was I entranced by them? Yes, I was. Their comedy was cross-talking, domestic short sketches, gags from newspapers, comic songs, crossing gags.'

Despite his enthusiasm, Mr O'Gorman wasn't for a moment permitted to even consider following in their footsteps. 'My father said under no circumstances should I consider it. It was too chancy even if you had any talent, which I hadn't. It was too chancy and too demanding and too uncertain, and at the time variety was coming to an end. He had a very sensible view of it all.'

But there was clearly something in the blood. Mr O'Gorman's career has been in teaching, but he has been an avid theatre-goer all his life and is a member of the British Music Hall Society. He says his book is an attempt to preserve what is in danger of being forgotten and to convey the lost atmosphere of the variety theatre. 'The variety artiste aimed to please, to provide amusement for those seeking a few hours' diversion, to enter a theatre and come out smiling, laughing or even singing a song they had just heard.'

[15 April 1999]

Such Happy Memories of Clowning around Archie, Bognor's very own Laughing Policeman

Whoever said a policeman's lot is not a happy one? Archie Greenshields, more than 26 years a Sussex policeman, would probably disagree. After all, he spent quite a lot of that time clowning. Mention Archie Oddsox to one-time children now of a certain age, and they'll know exactly who you mean. Archie, who lives in Bognor Regis, joined up in 1946 at a time when East and West Sussex constabularies were still separate. He soon discovered he had hidden talents.

Where there's Archie, there's laughter … Worthing, c.1970.

It all started when he joined the police's safety first team as a stuntman in a number of displays as to how not to drive and cycle. Archie was the poor cyclist on the receiving end of demonstrations designed to show what happens if you aren't considerate to other road users. Archie consequently took a series of tumbles – some rather more painful than others.

There was no training as such. It was the kind of job you just fell into. But the end result was that it gave Archie a taste for entertaining. Over the years he served in a succession of locations including Bognor Regis, Chichester, Worthing, Petworth and Rustington. And over the years his reputation as an entertainer grew.

'Early on, when I was at the station at Worthing, it was suggested that, during races, we would entertain the children by clowning. I did trick cycle-riding with the axle off-centre so that it went up and down, or trick cycling with the handlebars coming off.' He graduated to

Archie delights the children at the annual party organised by the police in Bognor Regis, 1973.

become a panto horse, going around entertaining the children. More fun followed when the superintendent in charge of the division held theme balls – Spanish, French, Japanese and so on. 'For the Spanish theme it was suggested we had a mock bullfight. I hired a cow costume from a theatrical emporium in Brighton. I became the back end and another colleague took the front end. We had a toreador as well. … Unfortunately things went a bit haywire. The chap who was doing the front of my bull had too much to drink and collapsed, knocking over tables and guests. I got out of my end to help him up!'

When Archie, now 78, went to Petworth station, he used to help out with children's parties. When he was moved to Bognor, he continued in much the same vein. To hundreds of children he was Mr Oddsox, helped on by a colourful costume featuring trilby hat plus red and white baggy trousers made for him by his wife. He also had an emu, but this was the time when the late Rod Hull and his emu were hitting the big time, so Archie's emu was an ostrich.

After he retired, Archie continued to clown, going to children's parties to entertain across the area. The secret of his success was that he would get down to the children's level and try to look at the world through children's eyes. He would get the children to play popular party games. While he was still working, his clowning took up pretty well all his rest days and all his weekends. The demand was ever increasing. Sometimes, however, things did go awry. Archie always made a point of arriving in costume as part of the illusion. After getting the booking from the parents, he would write to the child to say that his circus was in town, that he had heard they had a birthday and could he pop in.

One day he turned up, in clown's costume, on the wrong doorstep. 'The poor woman was so astonished she nearly had a stroke when she saw me!'

[2 September 1999]

Folk Song Club – One of the Great Survivors

It was only nine years old at the time, but it still counted 'as one of (the) country's oldest' when in 1970 the *Chichester Observer* warned of its possible demise. But, unlike so many, Chichester Folk Song Club didn't go under. Instead it has struggled on, through good times and not so good – one of the great survivors on the folk scene. As a result, its 40th anniversary this year finds it in good heart. Club organiser Marilyn Campbell has been a key player throughout most of those years. 'The club started because of the Martlet Morris Men,' Marilyn recalls. 'They used to have a Thursday evening dance. Some of them were singers and they would sing after their gatherings. The singing got more and more popular.' From this developed a weekly folk club at *The Hole In The Wall* – and so Chichester Folk Song Club was born.

Dick Mann, Ron Coe and Paul Morris were instrumental at the start, Marilyn recalls. 'Back then you had the folk revival all over the place. I remember Martin Carthy, one of the biggest names on the folk scene, said you could do a tour all week in the same town folk was so popular. My understanding is that the folk revival started in the early '50s'.

Above: *Chalky Corkrey, guest at Chichester Folk Song Club in 1983.*

Right: *Together they were Harvest … Marilyn Campbell, Spokey Wheeler and Miggy Rugg perform at Chichester's* Hole in the Wall *for Chichester Folk Song Club, 1970.*

Chichester Folk Club started in 1961 and was immediately affiliated to the national folk society. And even though scores of folk clubs have since closed, Marilyn insists that the folk revival continues apace, with the baton being passed to the next generation of performers.Chichester Folk Song Club has monthly guest performers, but mostly the emphasis is on participation – and that's the big attraction. The club boasts its own songwriters. It also boasts a wide-ranging interest. 'The club started by having a traditional base, but on any night there will be a good range of folk music with people of all ages coming along.' Marilyn admits she first got involved almost by chance – but she was soon hooked. 'I was in Brighton and there was nothing else to do. This was 1968 and I saw a Sussex folk evening advertised. It was the Copper family who are still active on the scene, and there were other musicians. We went in on the off-chance, and I was just fascinated by the songs and by the performance.'

Chichester Folk Song Club Mummies in 1992.

She also loved the fact that you could get talking to the performers. She was told that there was a folk scene back in Chichester: 'One of the performers said "do you know there is a folk club at *The Hole In The Wall*?" I have been going ever since.' It is clearly something that either grabs or it doesn't. Marilyn's two friends with whom she went enjoyed the evening but have never been back.

Over the years, the club enjoyed a spell at *The Fountain* in South Street before moving in search of a bigger venue to *The Gribble* at Oving. The point, as far as Marilyn is concerned, is that the club has always kept going. Sometimes numbers have dwindled to a point where other clubs might well have given up, but she has always taken the view that even if you have got just 17 people there, then that's still 17 people who will have had a good time. And that's how Chichester has managed to keep the folk flag flying ...

At the moment, things are fine, with a nice, steady core. And as Marilyn says, the club is comfortably dispelling the chunky sweater, finger-in-the-ear myth of the folk fan, the perfect image of someone rooted in the past and hankering for the days when life was simpler.

That's not the way it is, Marilyn insists. The health of the club is in the range of people and range of ages the club brings in. It doesn't look back. As Marilyn says, it most definitely looks forward.

[8 November 2001]

Chapter Nine

A NEW THEATRE IS BORN

The man who made it possible ... Chichester Festival Theatre founder, Leslie Evershed-Martin.

Building the Dream

Its first season in 1962 included the likes of Laurence Olivier, Keith Michell, Joan Plowright, Joan Greenwood, Fay Compton, Sybil Thorndike and Michael Redgrave.

Two years later, a stunning *Othello* boasted Olivier in the title role, Derek Jacobi as Cassio, Frank Finlay as Iago and Maggie Smith as Desdemona. It all seemed like it was meant to be ...

Chichester artist David Goodman was at the heart of the move to found Chichester Festival Theatre and he remembers still the exciting times. 'Leslie Evershed-Martin watched Tyrone Guthrie on TV talking about the theatre at Stratford, Ontario, and he thought, why shouldn't we do it here? He gathered a small group of mostly local people around him. Lord Bessborough was one of them, and soon after he suggested that I should join them. This was about 1959 or 1960. We used to meet in the Elizabethan room above the old *Punch House* by the Cross, and the conversation was about how we could raise the money to get the theatre going.

'It was extremely exciting and we lobbied all sorts of people. I became the honorary secretary of the group and did all the literature. There was enormous excitement. We produced lots of leaflets. I remember one of them was titled "How you can help this exciting adventure".

'Leslie was indefatigable at lobbying people including theatre people and all sorts of wealthy people including Paul Getty. ... We had many functions here and in London, and a London committee was formed under Teddy Smith who later became chairman of the board here. We had art exhibitions, an Arundel ball attended by Princess Alexandra who was a great supporter. It's an endless story.

'One of the things we would do was go around talking about the theatre as a way of trying to raise money for it. I did a lot of it and Leslie, of course, was the chief person. ... Leslie asked me to talk to the Townswomen's Guild at Wembley Town Hall because he couldn't go. I took a model of the theatre, but I lost my way and arrived late and instead of finding a small group found a thousand women and a Lord Mayor and a great stage.'

Looking back, Mr Goodman recalls the instant enthusiasm which infected people as soon as they learnt of the idea. 'We projected the idea that in theory it was impossible have a national theatre in what was then considered a small historic backwater, but in fact it became possible because Leslie was obviously undaunted and pushed everyone in front of him to make sure that it happened.'

[4 January 1996]

Her Royal Highness Princess Alexandra of Kent does the honours at the laying of the Chichester Festival Theatre's foundation stone.

Getting it off the Ground

Eileen Norris speaks with huge enthusiasm about that momentous opening season at Chichester Festival Theatre 40 years ago this year. Listen to her for a moment, and it's difficult not to share her excitement.

Top London actors were taking a great leap into the unknown. The venture was perilous. It was also thrilling ...

Eileen, who lives in Portsmouth, was in Chichester for that first 1962 season. She returned for the 1964 season as well. She had seen the earthmovers at work in Oaklands Park when the theatre was being built; she recalls seeing the theatre before the seats went in.

By the time the CFT opened its doors, Eileen had been brought down by the then general manager Pieter Rogers as an unofficial assistant stage manager. These were days when it was virtually impossible for women to get jobs in directing; the post of unofficial ASM was a foot in the door for Eileen. She soon saw how big a risk the whole venture was for Laurence Olivier as the first artistic director; she also saw just why he was the right man to take it on. Olivier had represented England in the film of *Henry V*. 'It was done in the 1940s and it was like Britain saying "yes, we are standing against the world and we are going to win!"' Olivier went on to do a number of great productions at the New Theatre in the 1940s. He did *Richard III* there before it became a film.

'He was the prime candidate to be the director of the National Theatre whenever that came about. We had been talking about the theatre, and the theatre seemed to represent so much of what Britain stood for. Olivier needed not so much to prove himself as a director, but he needed to get a great company around him, and that is what Chichester represented. But what a peril!'

Like Peggy Ashcroft, he was part of the new wave that had gone into the Royal Court, a place lots of established names wouldn't go near. It was a great breeding ground for talent. Olivier built on that work at Chichester.

Above: Eileen Norris, who recalls the huge excitement of those early days at Chichester Festival Theatre.

Right: Eileen Norris as she is today.

Below: A new theatre is born.

CHICHESTER

festival **THEATRE**

First Season 1962
July 3rd.–September 8th.

Director LAURENCE OLIVIER

LEWIS CASSON   FAY COMPTON
JOAN GREENWOOD   ROSEMARY HARRIS
KATHLEEN HARRISON   KEITH MICHELL
ANDRE MORELL   JOHN NEVILLE
LAURENCE OLIVIER   JOAN PLOWRIGHT
MICHAEL REDGRAVE   ATHENE SEYLER
SYBIL THORNDIKE   PETER WOODTHORPE

BOX OFFICE. Telephone CHICHESTER 4183 or tickets through the usual agencies

Prices from: 5/- (UNRESERVED) to 25/-

'My job was to look after the people here,' Eileen recalls. 'They could not afford a large cast of ASMs, but they needed someone to make the coffee and the tea.' The company wouldn't tolerate anyone watching rehearsals, but Pieter suggested that making the drinks was exactly the way in Eileen needed.

'He said "I can't afford to pay you", but watching is just the best way to learn. By making the tea, I had everyone coming to talk to me, and they would relax. They would talk, and those wonderful little jewels would drip from their lips – jewels about acting and technique. It was wonderful. It was a marvellous experience.'

The opening season opened with *The Chances*, a play which demanded a huge company with enormous costumes. The production worked well, but not at first.

'They set it up originally with blue light. But you can't open a comedy in blue light. It makes everybody cold and they won't laugh. So they had to reset the lighting. ... *The Chances* was marvellous fun, but was unfamiliar to the audience. But it used the theatre. That was the production's great strength. It was not necessarily an audience-puller, but I think on the whole the audience was there. It was a great company. It was a star-studded company.'

The next play was *The Broken Heart*, a piece about patrician values and the nobility of the ancient classical world: 'But it went terribly wrong. The set was painted and was enormous. The first time I saw the actors put their costumes on, I could see that they had difficulty matching the image they had of the parts to the costumes they had.'

It was also Olivier's first appearance on the stage, and he was terrified. Eileen remembers him saying of the audience 'They are so close!'.

'They had never had an audience so close before.' But Olivier gave a remarkable performance – all part of what Eileen calls his bravery as an actor: 'He could hold a pause better than anyone I have ever seen. In holding the pause, you get anticipation. There was a frisson of excitement when he stood there. He was terrific in *The Broken Heart*, but overall it was not a successful production.'

One problem was the lack of air-conditioning, particularly during a scene in which John Neville has his arms held out and is put to death by being bled from his wrists. The drip, drip of the blood was simulated. The combination of heat and horror was too much for some people. Eileen, by now in charge of the usherettes, remembers quite a few people passing out.

111

But then *Uncle Vanya* saved the season – a momentous production for the theatre. The box office was closed on Sundays, but Eileen remembers having to come in and set up a table to take bookings. People would sleep out at the theatre in the hope of getting a ticket.

The opening scene suggested what had changed. 'Sybil Thorndike is on the stage feeding chickens. Larry enters. He comes up to her very quietly and slaps her on the back … At last the actors were at home on the stage. It was relaxed. The tension had gone.'

Chichester Festival Theatre was on its way …

[28 February 2002]

When 'King' Olivier reigned

Imagine if Tom Cruise or Tom Hanks were suddenly appointed artistic director of the Chichester Cinema at New Park. What would be your response? The same, presumably, as met the announcement of Laurence Olivier's appointment as Chichester Festival Theatre's first director. It's too easy to look back now on the appointment as a fact of history. The passage of time has dimmed its impact and the excitement it generated. But take a look at the Laurence Olivier archive at the British Library, and you get the distinct impression of a Chichester hardly daring to believe its good fortune. Olivier, king among actors, was at the peak of his powers, a man in huge demand. Yet here he was in Chichester, at a theatre barely born.

Chichester Festival Theatre founder Leslie Evershed-Martin famously entitled his books on the CFT *The Impossible Theatre* and *The Miracle Theatre*. The Laurence Olivier archive, bought for the nation last year, suggests the extent to which these adjectives were well chosen. Across several hundred letters over almost five years, the Chichester section of the archive captures the daring of the moment; the thrill of a bold new chapter in British theatre.

The letters also suggest the inevitable tensions. Among the hopes are the worries. There is a sense of adventure, and with the adventure comes a sense of risk. But the letters also make it clear that Chichester believed it held the ace. And that ace was Olivier himself. No one was underestimating his importance to the whole undertaking. As the theatre contemplates its third season, Evershed-Martin writes to Olivier: 'I doubt whether you can possibly realise how much your actual presence during the last two seasons in Chichester has created a feeling of trust and confidence in everybody that Chichester was of importance in the theatrical world.' Pieter Rogers, general manager, writes to Olivier in January 1964: 'The only point I would like to raise with you urgently is the question of performances of *Othello*. It is so

Stars of the present and stars of the future line up for the first season at Chichester Festival Theatre.

CHICHESTER
festival THEATRE
Box Office Chichester 4183

FIRST SEASON - JULY 3rd until SEPTEMBER 8th

directed by LAURENCE OLIVIER

LEWIS CASSON	FAY COMPTON	JOAN GREENWOOD
ROSEMARY HARRIS		KATHLEEN HARRISON
KEITH MICHELL	ANDRE MORELL	JOHN NEVILLE
LAURENCE OLIVIER	JOAN PLOWRIGHT	MICHAEL REDGRAVE
ATHENE SEYLER	SYBIL THORNDIKE	PETER WOODTHORPE

GENE ANDERSON   TIMOTHY BATESON   ARTHUR BROUGH
ALAN HOWARD   ROBERT LANG

POLLY ADAMS   BETH BOYD   ELIZABETH BURGER   PATRICIA CONOLLY   ROWENA COOPER
LAWRENCE DAVIDSON   KENNETH EDWARDS   DAVID FUTCHER   DAPHNE GODDARD   RICHARD HAMPTON
JANET HENFREY   VALERIE HERMANNI   WILLIAM HOBBS   TERENCE KNAPP
ROBIN PHILLIPS   ADAM ROWNTREE   JOSEPHINE STUART   DANVERS WALKER

THE CHANCES
a comedy by JOHN FLETCHER, adapted by the Duke of Buckingham
decor by Malcolm Pride, music by Herbert Menges, dances arranged by Eleanor Fazan
Evenings 7-15 July 4, 5, 6, 7, 13, 23, 25, 27. August 9, 11, 13, 15, 17, 21, 30. September 1, 3, 5, 7.
Matinees 2-15 July 14, 21. August 2, 4, 8, 23, 28, 29.

THE BROKEN HEART
a tragedy by JOHN FORD   decor by ROGER FURSE, music by John Addison, dances arranged by Eleanor Fazan
Evenings 7-15 July 10, 11, 12, 14, 20, 24. August 2, 4, 6, 8, 10, 14, 23, 25, 27, 29, 31. September 4.
Matinees 2-15 July 12, 26, 28. August 1, 16, 18, 22. September 6, 8.

UNCLE VANYA
scenes from country life by ANTON CHEKHOV, translated by Constance Garnett
designed by Sean Kenny, costumes by Beatrice Dawson
Evenings 7-15 July 17, 18, 19, 21, 26, 28, 30. August 1, 3, 7, 16, 18, 20, 22, 24, 28. September 6.
Matinees 2-15 July 19, 25. August 9, 11, 15, 30. September 1, 8.

Joan Plowright, among the stars in Chichester Festival Theatre's very first season.

Sir Laurence Olivier, a key figure in the first seasons at the new Chichester Festival Theatre.

vital, I feel, from the point of view of the box office that you appear in as many performances in *Othello* as you can . . . from the box office angle alone, we know that when you appear in a classic, we are virtually sold out before we start.' There is a sense of the awe in which Olivier is held. Rogers adds: 'I am so deeply sorry to bother you over this when you must be up to your eyes in preparation for the role, but I felt it only right to let you know how much we feel we need you in Chichester this coming season.' Rogers asks Olivier to commit to at least 21 or 22 of the 62 or 63 performances in Chichester.

Olivier's reply underlines both his importance and his awareness of the risks involved (February 1964): 'I very much appreciate the desire of the Board to have me give as many performances of *Othello* as possible but as usual, my dear, they don't know what they are asking for. Nobody has tried to do a great Shakespeare role in this theatre. Whatever else we may have tried, we know it is twice as hard to do it here than in any other theatre. That's all we know.'

Later that year, Olivier was reassured, writing to Evershed-Martin that the season 'did allay certain fears – I know you had none, but I had several – concerning a Shakespearean production.'

Anxiety is a frequent tone in the letters in the archive. Rogers (early 1964) writes pressing Olivier to give the go-ahead to open booking for the season. The precariousness of the venture is also underlined in correspondence as the theatre's second season looms. Evershed-Martin writes to Olivier in May 1963 to tell him that the confidence of the board had been 'very shaken' by Olivier's budgets which show a possible loss of £9,000 even if the theatre plays to 75 per cent capacity. 'Whilst it is obviously too late to do anything about the cost of the productions, we do hope you will do your very utmost for us to increase the income of the theatre by the sale of any of the productions to other theatres or television rights.

'With an unknown play, it seems very likely that we might not get more than 75 per cent capacity and I am sure you know that if there is a deficit it will fall to the guarantors for £1,000 each and that whilst some can well afford it, others like myself simply cannot.' But Olivier has confidence in his season which includes *Saint Joan* and *The Workhouse Donkey*. He tells Evershed-Martin: 'I don't honestly think there is a cause for either of us to get into a state of absolute panic. Last year we played to a higher capacity than 75 per cent, and I think perhaps it is a little harsh to bring present-year possibilities down to 75 per cent particularly in view of the fact that our booking at the moment is exactly double that which it was at this precise moment last year.' Olivier comes up with the reasons for the more expensive season ahead – more directors than in the inaugural season, and royalties up threefold. Olivier then goes through the projections, adding: 'All of these figures are pretty stupid, dear Leslie, because as you have gathered by now in the theatre, one never knows until one knows.'

[22 February 2001]

113

Home is where the Art is for Michael

Chichester electrician Michael Elphick wanted a career in acting. Fortunately, he was in the right place to make the switch. Not many people – certainly not many electricians – can claim to have taken their early guidance from Laurence Olivier. But such good fortune fell to Elphick.

And it has been guidance which has stood him in good stead ever since. Michael has gone on to become a household name, thanks in large part to his performance in the title role of ITV's phenomenally successful Boon. He has also enjoyed a distinguished stage career.

Michael, who was born in Chichester, recalls he'd been in a few plays at school.

'I went to the secondary modern, the Lancastrian it was called then. So I was in these plays, and it was something that I thought I could do. But being a secondary modern, there was no way I could get a reasonable response from the teachers about being an actor.

'It was something that was regarded as a bit odd. I did have one teacher who encouraged me, and his name was Stubbs,' recalls Michael. 'He was involved with the Chichester Amateur Dramatic Society and got me in a play called *The Lady's not for Burning* that we performed at the Assembly Rooms in North Street. I was about 15 years old at the time. That was the year they were building this new theatre in Chichester. I often used to go up there to watch them building it.

'I had a paper round and part of my round was Franklin Place, so from there I could see the theatre going up. And then I left school, having done not very well, and got a job on the site just navvying. I was then taken on as an apprentice electrician working on the lights, which is when I met Laurence Olivier.

'Olivier directed a lot of the early stuff so he did the lighting plots and, as I was working with the electrics crew, I got to know him more than the actors.'

Workmen and guests gather for the topping-out ceremony at the new theatre.

Sir Laurence Olivier, Leslie Evershed-Martin, guests and workmen enjoy the topping-out ceremony at Chichester Festival Theatre.

Sir Laurence Olivier and Leslie Evershed-Martin discuss the detail of the new theatre.

At Chichester, Michael worked with such actors as Derek Jacobi, Robert Stephens, Frank Finlay and Joan Plowright.

He even trod the boards as a non-speaking extra. 'In *St Joan* I walked on as a guard and stood with her while that enormously long scene with the Inquisitor goes on. I had to stand absolutely still for 20 minutes.'

Olivier, however, remained the principal inspiration. 'He was a very approachable man. He had absolutely no airs or graces. I asked him several times what to do to get into acting and he said get some audition speeches together. He gave me three speeches to learn – Bottom from *A Midsummer Night's Dream*, the opening speech from *Under Milk Wood* and John Osborne's *Epitaph for George Dillon*.'

Michael went to London and auditioned for the four main drama schools, including RADA, and was offered places at all of them. RADA was considered 'it' at the time, but Michael went instead for the Central School of Speech and Drama. His reason, quite simply, was that this was where Olivier had studied.

Ten years, later Michael worked with Olivier on television. 'I was terrified that he wouldn't remember me. But immediately I walked into the rehearsal room he said "Michael, how are you?" He was a great man – a truly great man.' It was many years, however, before Michael returned to his home stage. A couple of years ago, he was at Chichester Festival Theatre in a touring production of Eric Chappell's comedy *It Can Damage Your Health*. Now he is back again – this time in the touring version of the Festival Theatre's production of Joe Orton's *Loot*. It will be at the CFT this spring. The play was one of the hits of last year's summer season, playing to packed houses in the Minerva before transferring to London. It's now been recast, with Michael in the role of the inspector, and it's visiting Chichester as part of an 18-week tour of the country. *Loot*'s return to Chichester will be a must for all those who saw it here last year.

[25 February 1999]

115

Magical days working with Olivier

The yellowing pages of a 36-year-old copy of the *Chichester Observer* are a reminder of the small but exciting role Janet Henfrey played in the very earliest days of Chichester Festival Theatre. Janet, who is currently on stage at the CFT in the summer season opener *Saturday, Sunday … and Monday*, was a member of Laurence Olivier's first-ever company at the fledgling Festival Theatre in 1962.

It was her second job in the theatre, and she got it after three auditions, the last before Olivier himself. Her reward was to understudy for both *The Chances* and *The Broken Heart*, though sadly she got to go on only for the dress rehearsal.

'But it was absolutely magical,' she recalls. 'For anybody starting out their work in the theatre to work with such giants as we had was wonderful.

'It gave you such a sense of purpose and such a sense of dedication to something much bigger than any single individual. These were people who felt such passion for what they were doing. It was a great lesson to learn.

'It was marvellous to hear Sybil Thorndike talking about her love for the project – which is not an easy word to bandy around, even in those days. What it gave me was a beacon as to what theatre can and should be.'

The creation of Chichester Festival Theatre was a major talking point. 'Theatres on that scale aren't exactly built very often, even in the 1960s when there was a great optimism for the arts. It was something very special. Olivier then went on to found the National Theatre.'

Keith Michell returned to the theatre to star in Monsieur Amilcar *with Penelope Keith in 1995. Michell was in Chichester Festival Theatre's first ever season and later returned as artistic director.*

Chichester Festival Theatre under construction.

There was a great sense of excitement at Chichester – despite conditions which were decidedly less than primitive.

'There was a famous occasion when somebody walking his dog in the park wandered on to the back of the stage. It was all open at the back. It was still being built around us.'

The current production is Janet's first time back on the CFT stage since that very first season. 'One follows in a general sense everything that goes on in the theatre, but Chichester has always been rather special. … Its disadvantage is that it has such a big auditorium to fill, and it is a theatre which has gone through very troubled times in the past year. … But I hope what we are seeing is the beginning of a renaissance for the theatre. It is such a wonderful asset socially and educationally.'

She admits certain things need to happen before it can fully flourish again: 'It needs to be more user-friendly to the young and to have more ticket prices for the young.'

But ultimately it lies in the hands of the people of Chichester whether the theatre can rebuild: 'We need people to come along and support the theatre.'

[18 June 1998]

Sir Laurence and the Dirty Nappy

A treasured souvenir of a celebrated inaugural season. Eileen Norris' signed cast list from the 1962 season. Timothy Bateson featured in two of the plays.

Timothy Bateson remembers he was changing a nappy when the call came through. It was a particularly fruity nappy.

'The voice said "My name is Pieter Rogers, the general manager. Sir Laurence would like a word with you." Sir Laurence Olivier came on, and he said "Timmy, dear boy, what are you doing?" I had the nappy with contents in my hands and I said so. Sir Laurence said "Don't be a fool. I mean what are you doing? Would you like to come to Chichester?"'

Timothy answered yes and so joined the company for the first-ever season at Chichester Festival Theatre. He appeared in *The Chances* and *The Broken Heart*. 'My relationship with Sir Laurence was never close but I had worked with him before, and because he was Sir Laurence he could get whoever he wanted for his cast. The place was packed every night. An enormous number of people would come not only from London, but from all around England. There was such glamour to it all, and that's what the theatre needs to do now – to really draw on the locality here and the wider locality.'

Timothy is now back in Chichester in the cast of *Chimes At Midnight*, appearing on the CFT stage for the first time since that 1962 season.

'It's tremendously important that we do all we can to work with the city and the people here. Otherwise they will think that there is this strange building in Oaklands Park, but they don't know what goes on in there.

'Sir Laurence said at the time that we had to face the fact that a large number of citizens of Chichester would have preferred a swimming pool on the site. He encouraged us to go around and talk to people and to get them interested.

'There was some big do with the mayor. Sir Laurence said to us to be very sweet and to make sure that we got there on time and was there anyone who could lend him a pair of decent trousers. A young man in fact lent him a suit, and he has done very well in the profession as a result!'

Sir Laurence was the absolute figurehead, Timothy recalls.

'We were all besotted with the man. He was so electrifying to work with. I think he had an understanding of the power and the importance of acting above everything else in the theatre. It's not to do with getting inside the skin. It's to do with acting.

'He got rid of the false and the phoney, and he was a great, great actor. I would do anything he said. We totally believed in him. The rehearsals were quite extraordinary. He directed three plays, playing the lead in two and opened them all in ten days.

'One of the actors did try to alter a move. Sir Laurence said "I have sweated my guts out for months over the blocking. This may be wrong but would you just try it?" And in fact not a single move had to be changed for all the three plays.

'As for performance, you can't define what it is that makes an audience just not able to take their eyes off an actor. Even when he was being less than good, it was totally riveting stuff.'

[6 August 1998]

Thrilling Theatre Days with Laurence Olivier

Actress Polly Adams' stint in *The Winslow Boy* at Chichester Festival Theatre is bringing back happy memories of the theatre's first-ever season 39 years ago. 'It was only tiny roles – like a handmaiden in *The Broken Heart* and a whore and a citizen in *The Chances*,' Polly recalls. But these were exciting days – the birth of a brand-new theatre, with Laurence Olivier, no less, at the helm.

Polly Adams enjoyed the excitement of the early days at Chichester Festival Theatre.

Polly was born in Itchenor and still lives in the house she was born in: 'I went and lived in London from being a drama student onwards.' But the family connection remained: 'We nearly sold the house just after my mother died but I gave up living in London and came down here full-time. I have never regretted it.'

Back in those early days of the CFT's first season, Polly used to cycle in from Itchenor. She passed her driving test during the summer. It was a dream job: 'I went and auditioned for Sir Laurence and I was accepted.' One of her duties was as an understudy for Sir Laurence's wife, Joan Plowright, though, sadly for Polly, she was never called on to step up.

Even so, though her roles were small, she was still caught up in the excitement of it all. She well remembers the fund-raising which preceded the theatre's opening. 'I was away living in London by then. Actors are generally London-based, but all the same one was absolutely thrilled at what was happening. We were all so excited at this new project. It was absolutely thrilling.

'Sir Laurence was leading the company. I suppose I took it for granted that it would be a success. I don't think I thought in terms of success, actually. I think I just thought in terms of being so excited and working with Sir Laurence and of having the chance to watch him at close quarters.

'He was so generous to all of us. We felt like we were his children. We even called him "dad" – though not to his face because he was formidable as well. One felt a bit paralysed when he came to give notes. You would say to your friends afterwards "What did he say? I didn't take it all in!"

'One was just mesmerised by his extraordinary presence. But I tried to listen very much to him. All I know is that at the end of the season, he wrote us all letters really criticising – I mean, constructively – us as actors and giving us advice. … Each of us got a very considered and helpful letter. I remember to me he said "You must be very careful to develop as an actress because you might get stuck playing very English parts" because I was rather stiff and buttoned-up as an actress in those days.

'I think I was quite carefree as a person, but he felt I needed to loosen up more as an actress. I thought it was such a great thing to do, that he should have bothered to tell us these things.'

[21 June 2001]

Memories of the Great and the Good

Frank Finlay, who last night opened in *The Handyman* in the Minerva Theatre, finds Chichester a place full of memories.

Frank, a dastardly Captain Hook in the Festival Theatre's Christmas production a couple of years ago, goes right back to the Festival Theatre's very earliest days. In 1963 he appeared in Shaw's *Saint Joan* in a cast including Joan Plowright, Robert Stephens, Jeremy Brett, Derek Jacobi and Norman Rossington. *The Workhouse Donkey* also saw him alongside Stephens, Brett, Jacobi, and Rossington.

The following year, *The Dutch Courtesan* saw him on stage with Billie Whitelaw and John Stride, and also as Iago to Olivier's Othello in a mouth-watering cast which boasted Jacobi as Cassio, Maggie Smith as Desdemona, Edward Petherbridge as a senate officer and Edward Hardwicke as Montano.

Even now Frank relishes the sense of excitement which surrounded the fledgling theatre.

Frank Finlay pictured during the 1963 season.

'*Saint Joan* and *The Workhouse Donkey* were the second season, and it was wonderful. It was so exciting when we were all asked to go to Chichester. ... Olivier had started the first season with *Uncle Vanya*, and between him doing the first and the second he was offered the directorship of the National. ... The second season was really a try-out for lots of actors. It was Olivier's way of preparing himself for running a company for the National.'

Maybe about a half or two thirds of that company went on to become founder members of the National. 'You really did feel that it was the beginning of everything. There was a great sense of expectation.'

Things have obviously moved on since then, and for Chichester too. ... 'Chichester seemed quieter in those days. It was still very much the kind of place that people came to for the summer. It had a wonderful feeling about it, and there was a lot of hospitality given to us.' Members of the summer season company all played in at least a couple of the plays, and many of the actors had young families. 'My children were then four or five years old and eight or nine years old, and in that second year there was a lot of to-ing and fro-ing to London.

'Once the children's holidays had started we could come to Chichester as much as we wanted. I stayed in Bosham one year and in Selsey the next year. There were lots of children around and it was the most marvellous family feel to the whole thing.'

Frank admits it all seems a long time ago now, but the passing years haven't dimmed his admiration for Olivier. Olivier's contribution wasn't just to Chichester. It was to the National and to the world of acting in general, Frank is quick to insist. But those Chichester days were special indeed. 'I worked with him over many many years. We did a lot of plays together and we worked on television. I was devoted to him both as a man and as an actor.'

[19 September 1996]

Carping, Coughing and 'Dearest Danski'

Try to conjure a theatrical name today of the same standing Laurence Olivier enjoyed in the early 1960s. Difficult. And it's even more difficult to imagine him or her writing the kind of letter Olivier wrote as a matter of course while at Chichester as the first director of the Festival Theatre in the early '60s.

A member of the audience wrote to Sir Laurence in 1963 to complain that some of the actors were inaudible. Olivier replied personally. 'There

Derek Jacobi featured in the 1963 season. He returned in 1995 as the theatre's artistic director.

is one thing I feel bound to mention in defence of the cast and that is that often the coughing in audiences makes it seem as though the actors are inaudible and the actors are aware of this inaudibility and not of the fact that they themselves are the cause.'

The letter, one among hundreds in Laurence Olivier's personal archive which has just been opened to public scrutiny for the first time, shows the depth of 'Larry's' involvement in Chichester's fledgling theatrical project. Another letter to Olivier (August 1965) complains that the intervals between acts are far too short and that they contain too many reminders about how long to go until the performance resumes. Sadly, Olivier's response doesn't seem to have survived. But again the letter suggests the hands-on manner of the CFT's first director. Olivier was clearly a hoarder and his CFT memorabilia fill a substantial box, one of 180 acquired for the nation last year by the British Library. The box contains early-season guides, from the days when tickets ranged in price from £1 to £1.50. The collection even includes a batch of architects' plans for the theatre sent to Olivier in October 1961.

A royal visitor to Chichester Festival Theatre in the 1960s ... Her Royal Highness the Queen Mother.

Also included are his heavily-annotated scripts for the first couple of seasons. His copy of *The Chances*, for instance, contains Olivier's diagrams of on-stage movements on virtually every page. Olivier's home-made tabs down the side guide him to particular scenes.

There is also a book of notes into which he pours his thoughts, along with notes for directing. 'Then it is a question of concentration, conviction (if you don't believe it, why should the audience?)' is one particular spur to performance. Another is the note: 'If you scratch your nose, see that it is a charming gesture.' Among the letters, many suggest an easy informality. Frequently Olivier is apologising for not having seen somebody. More often than not, it's the theatre's founder Leslie Evershed-Martin to whom he is saying sorry. He writes in September 1964: 'I seem to be putting you off and putting you off and it must almost seem to you that I am

Derek Jacobi made an unhappy return to the Festival Theatre stage in the 1996 production of Love for Love. *He was forced to pull out just before the opening night after being taken ill with appendicitis.*

avoiding you. This you must know is not the case.' A few months later, he is apologising again, this time for not telling Evershed-Martin first of his decision to resign as director.

Elsewhere it is the day-to-day business of the theatre that is his concern, from seat reservations to telephone numbers, from staff appointments to thanks for the receipt of a set of caricatures.

Olivier also niggles that Goodwood is signposted around town by the AA, but the theatre isn't. Other correspondence deals with the possibility of filming a play at Chichester. And in January 1967 he is attempting to recruit Danny Kaye ('Dearest Danski') offering a 'wee word' of encouragement that Kaye should come to Chichester to do *A Servant of Two Masters*. 'Franco Zeffirelli says he would move heaven and earth to direct it for you if you would like that', he adds in a hand-written postscript.

[1 March 2001]

Chapter Ten

SPORTING FEATS AND THRILLS

Olympic Hopeful who ran just for Teenage Fun

Whit Monday Sports Day in Chichester's Priory Park was one of the highlights of the sporting calendar back in the 1950s. For Felpham woman Mrs Cicely Smith it was the scene of repeated triumph. The event dated back to Victorian days and by the time Mrs Smith, then Cicely Dance, took part it had reached a peak of popularity, regularly drawing crowds of more than 3,000 spectators.

The Women's Amateur Athletic Association Sussex County Championships were then an integral part of the day's sporting activities, and Mrs Smith, once touted as an Olympic hopeful, was soon clocking up an impressive record of success. She was the 100 and 150 yards Sussex Schools Champion in 1949 and 1950; came third in the 150 yards final of the England Schools Championship in 1950; was the 100 and 220 yards Sussex County Champion from 1952 to 1954 inclusive; and had a dead-heat with the existing British champion in the 100 yards at the National Championships in London in 1952.

Looking back, Mrs Smith, who lives in Felpham, remembers that there was just something inside her that made her run fast. By the age of 14 in 1949 she was the Westloats Lane School sprint champion and the Sussex Schools under-15 champion in 100 and 150 yards. And the victories just piled up from there.

But Mrs Smith insists it was all just a bit of fun: 'I would train twice a week, but I didn't take it all very seriously. It was the school that started it all.' In all, she enjoyed around six years at the top, stopping only when she got married and moved away from Bognor. 'It was hard work being a housewife in those days, with gas irons and no washing machines! The sport was just something I did for teenage fun.'

She says she doesn't regret giving it all up. Her one wish, though, would be to be a sprinter now. 'Now they have really superb tracks. And now that there is money involved I would go out of my way to make sure I took off.' Another advantage to running today would be not having to face the brutal finishing ropes which were used back in the 1950s.

A picture shows Mrs Smith just as the ecstasy of winning gives way to the agony of winning. The taut rope across her neck is just about to give her a cut which she remembers still to this day. 'I screamed like billy-oh. I cut my throat. I actually cut my neck by about six inches. It was absolutely ridiculous ...'

[6 February 1997]

123

Catching up on Life through Sport

Chichester's Ronald Howick always felt that the war had robbed him of six years of his life. That's one of the reasons he threw himself into sport with such vigour, reckons his son Peter. It was as if he was trying to catch up. 'In 1930 he was at the Central School for Boys winning an athletics cup,' Peter says. 'Ten years later, there he is in uniform in the war. Just ten years apart. It's incredible when you think of it.

'He went into the war when he was 24. I suppose he was looking forward to everything, and then the war came along. He would have come back when he was 30, and ever afterwards he was trying to make up for lost time. He played so much sport.'

Central School for Boys athletics team in 1930. Ronald Howick is on the far right.

Sport was a feature in his early life, too. Oddly, by his own high standards, sport, however, seemed one of his weaker cards on a school report for when he was eight years ten months.

Ronald (1916-87) collected a string of As for arithmetic, reading, composition, recitation, history, geography, handwriting, conduct, punctuality and attendance. Never late and never absent, he was top of the class, and his teacher adjudged him to have 'done very well indeed'. In physical training, however, he dipped out with a B. 'It's a bit surprising,' Peter says. 'If I had known, I would have had a go at him about it. I would have said "I thought you were good at sport!"

'But he was definitely very sports-loving. He was a very popular person in the sporting field. Everyone said "Good old Ron". But he was a little bad-tempered at times. He had his moments!

'But I must admit that you have got to admire someone who plays football until 50 and then cricket until nearly 60 and then takes up golf. He played football for Chichester City and Portfield. He was what they called wing half in those days – what they would call midfield today.

Ronald Howick's wedding to Molly at St Paul's Church, Chichester in 1940.

Ronald in his days as an aircraft fitter at RAF Tangmere.

'Towards the end of his career, I played two or three times with him. He was very good, but he was reluctant to play me. He was the manager and he would always want to find someone else. He didn't want any nepotism creeping into his side. ... He also used to play in goal. He even played in goal for the first team when they were short towards the end of the season. He would turn out anywhere. He was that sort of person.

'He played cricket for Rowes Hornets after the war. He was a batsman/wicketkeeper. And then he played for the Ivanhoe cricket club until he finished. He was an opening batsman. He was a reasonably quick-scorer. He didn't hang about. He had a good eye and he liked to get on with it.

'He never scored a hundred, but he got a lot of 50s. To get hundreds, you have to have a lot of concentration, and I think the fact that his temperament was what it was meant that he didn't stay there long enough. He wanted to score quickly and then think about keeping wicket, diving around later.

'He said to me that in those days – after the war – you could play cricket or football virtually every night of the week. He would just play any sport he could he was so keen – much to my mother's disgust!'

[27 May 1999]

Gunners Career, but Mother said 'No'

With probably something of an understatement, George Maslen recalls: 'I expect I had a few tears.' Even now, he still gets ribbed that he could have ended up as the manager of Arsenal if things had turned out differently. Who knows? But there seems little doubt that a career in professional football was beckoning at Highbury – if only his mother had said yes. But she didn't and, instead, George spent 37 years playing for Portfield Football Club in Chichester. One highlight was 33 goals in a season – though not the club record.

A certain Lenny Hide managed 65 in a season at the phenomenal rate of about two a game. Even so, George's was a distinguished career on the field. 'I first played for Portfield in 1933 when I was 13. I had to put my age up! I think you had to be 16 or 17 so I had to tell a lie.

'I had the chance to turn professional when I was 14. There was a nursery for the Arsenal. They came down to see my mother, but she would not let me go. Otherwise I would have been a professional. But my mother didn't think much of football. I expect I had a few tears. It was a big disappointment.'

George did once play for Sussex, but only once. 'I didn't play very well, and they never picked me any more.'

George's great strength was that he could kick with both feet. 'That was one of the big advantages. There are quite a few professionals playing today who can't kick with their left foot, but I was equally good with both.'

George played mainly at centre-half, but over the years he played in almost every position. He finally packed up when he wasn't far off 50 – the end of a long career for Portfield.

He says: 'I played one or two games for Chichester, but only when I was available. Portfield still exists at the moment, but it won't for much longer. The team is called Chichester City United now, but it is still Portfield as far as I am concerned.' Football is now very different from the game George played and saw in his heyday, but he admits he struggles to put his finger on just how it has changed. George belonged to the era of Stanley Matthews and Tom Finney, part of a footballing golden age.

He says: 'The one that I always used to like to watch was Stanley Matthews. A lot of people say he wasn't the best, but I can't see who was if he wasn't. George Best was near.

'I liked the way Matthews used to run down the wing and take the ball right to the byline and always bring it back. He always used to provide chances for the other players to score.

'Tom Finney was another one who was almost as good. He was a similar type to Matthews. He didn't dribble quite so much, but he was good at running very fast.'

[7 June 2001]

Referee's Proud Record

Former referee William Saunders can proudly claim to have been associated with the West Sussex football league for half of its 100-year history. The league reaches its centenary next year, by which time it will be exactly 50 years since Mr Saunders first ran out with his black shirt and whistle.

Mr Saunders, who is now researching a history of the league, remembers the heady immediate post-war days with affection. 'I was lucky. I got into the West Sussex league fairly quickly. Everybody wanted to get back. There had been some form of football during the war, but not a lot. Certainly the local leagues had been virtually disbanded.

'It all started up again in the 1946-47 season. Most of the chaps wanted to get back to the life they knew before the war, if that was possible. I had decided at school that I wanted to be a referee. It was just a hobby really. I was about 25 to 27 at the time and it was a lovely time.'

Mr Saunders' philosophy was simple: 22 players go out onto the pitch at the start of the game and at the end of it 22 players should

William Saunders at his desk at the Southern Electricity Board office in North Street, Chichester in the early 1950s. At the time he was the district order clerk.

William Saunders (in dark glasses) going on to the pitch at Torquay in the 1960s. At one time he was on the senior match committee of the Sussex County Football Association.

come back off. Refereeing was based on gaining respect and from that respect, liking would flow.

Mr Saunders stopped refereeing in 1962 and moved into administration, gaining election to the position of representative on the Sussex County Society of Referees. He has now been on the county FA for 36 years. Throughout those years, he has remained a close student of the game, and it's a game he reckons has changed remarkably little over the passing decades. Dissent has increased, but the laws of the game haven't altered greatly. One thing he laments, though, is an increase in negative defensive play. In the golden days football was all about scoring. Supporters would rather have seen their team go down 4-3 than come away with a nil-nil draw. Not something that would be the case now.

Mr Saunders also laments a certain loss of freedom in the game, something he believes could be easily remedied. He is against an increase of lines on the pitch because that would simply lead to confusion, but big benefits would follow from extending the 18-yard box to the sidelines. The new 18-yard sector would be the only area where off-side rules would apply, freeing up the centre of the pitch for a new creative approach which is currently stultified by over-use of off-side. Off-side should also cease to apply, he believes, when a free kick is awarded. The free kick is a punishment, but it's a punishment which can be severely mitigated if the offenders are allowed to counter it with an off-side trap.

[14 December 1995]

127

Tears of Pain and Joy

Not many mothers thumped their daughter in celebration of England's 1966 World Cup win. But at least life-long football fanatic Audrey Voller, of Newlands Lane, Chichester, can claim that it was accidental. 'I was watching the 1966 World Cup final with my daughter Nita and one of her friends,' she recalls. 'It was getting very exciting near the end of the match. ... I was up and down in my seat when Geoff Hurst scored the winning goal. I jumped up, threw my arms around and I hit Nita full force on the nose. She sat there crying with pain and I was crying with sheer delight. We had won the World Cup and had beaten Germany! We will both remember that day for the rest of our lives.'

Rooting for England: Audrey Voller.

Mrs Voller recalls that she had a good feeling about England's chances that year. Fortunately she's also got a good feeling about their chances this time round for the 1998 World Cup campaign. Mrs Voller is backing England to reach the semi-finals at least and is backing Shearer, Owen and Seaman as the key players.

As for the key players 32 years ago, Mrs Voller is in no doubt that it was hat-trick hero Hurst who was the player of the final. 'All the goals were fantastic, and I remember the oohs and ahhs of the crowd. It was a very emotional time for me – and for everyone else!' It was one of those days when everyone was right behind England, and the millions who weren't fortunate enough to be at Wembley were glued to their tellies.

'A few years later Bobby Moore came to Oaklands Park. I think there was a charity football match taking place. So I rushed down there hoping for a chance to see my hero. I met Bobby and had a chat. He was very nice. He picked up my son Paul, aged two, and he kissed him and said he hoped Paul would be a footballer one day.'

A pensioner now, Mrs Voller still goes to Wembley with her family to urge England on. 'We have our England shirts and all sing Football's Coming Home.' Whether it actually will, remains to be seen – but whatever happens at least Mrs Voller and her family have got the consolation of being Liverpool supporters.

The Liverpool trophies may have been fewer and further between in recent years, but Mrs Voller is convinced that the glory days for Liverpool, at least, aren't so far away.

[28 May 1998]

Cold War Tensions set aside for 90 Minutes

Charles Ayling has a very good reason for remembering exactly where he was when England won the World Cup in 1966. He was forced to listen to the match by the very people he was supposed to be spying on – a group of Russian soldiers anxious to hear the Germans lose. Mr Ayling had a working radio. The Russians didn't. And that made him a hot commodity in the darkest days of the Cold War.

Mr Ayling, of Shamrock Close, Chichester, was in the RAF at the time, stationed with The British Commander in Chief's Mission to the Soviet Forces in Germany – a posting recently acknowledged as one of Britain's most daring Cold War spying missions.

Charles Ayling, who was on one of Britain's most daring Cold War spying missions.

'I was on duty at the Mission House in Potsdam,' he recalls. 'The match had been on for about half an hour. I decided to go to West Berlin to pick up some kit. I was listening to the match on the car radio when I arrived at the Soviet check point. … A Soviet soldier took my pass to book me through. A Soviet officer came over to the car and told me they could not let me pass as their radio was unserviceable and they wanted to listen to the match hoping England would win.

'I had to stay there until the match finished and, as England had won, out came a bottle of vodka to celebrate. When my pass was finally returned to me, I went back to the Mission House having decided to give up the run to West Berlin.'

Glienicke Bridge, where Charles Ayling was stopped.

It wasn't until later that Mr Ayling actually got to see the goals, but he took away with him from his encounter the realisation that the

Russians really weren't as bad as people often made out. These were worrying days, not long after the wall had gone up. Tensions were high, but even though Mr Ayling didn't have much choice about sharing his radio, the Russians turned out to be quite reasonable people.

When the match went into extra time, Mr Ayling admits he feared a little for its outcome. But looking back now, he reckons that England really did have a world-beating side – something they haven't got now. 'They were footballers then. They put everything they had into it. They went out to win the cup and they did it.'

Since then, he says, money has spoilt the game. England tend to go for a goal lead and then sit back. In days gone by, the first goal would have been regarded as the signal to score more.

129

Mr Ayling reckons the England team should still do quite well in France in this year's World Cup campaign. He's backing them to get to the semi-finals, but he believes the finals are probably beyond them. One thing should help England, though, and that's the sending home of Gazza – the troubled Paul Gascoigne. 'The man is a fool to himself. He has had everything laid out for him, and he has just thrown it away. I don't think [England manager Glenn] Hoddle should have taken him out there in the first place. I think he is going to end up another George Best before he finishes.'

[4 June 1998]

World Cup Madness and Insults from Jagger

Quite often the fans would answer him back a bit; usually someone would flick his cap in a little gesture of mischievous disdain. But not on World Cup Final day 1966. No, that was the day everyone was wonderfully well behaved.

Not surprising, really. 'They were too frightened that they would get thrown out', Charles Dawson recalls. 'And they would have been!'

Charles, who lives in Bracklesham Bay, was in charge of the 200-strong body of commissionaires on that momentous day. His job was to help his fellow ex-servicemen keep order. It was a job which gave them all a ringside seat at one of the greatest moments in the annals of English sporting history.

A former sergeant in the Royal Marines, Charles became a sergeant-major with the Corps of Commissionaires, and with the Corps he attended every major football match at Wembley from around 1960 to 1980. He covered internationals and cup finals; also, at Wembley and elsewhere, he covered hundreds of pop concerts. On one famous occasion at a Rolling Stones gig, he led his band of ex-soldiers out in protest at a distinctly disparaging comment apparently made by Mick Jagger from the stage.

Charles was clearly not someone you would want to mess with. With his service background he had all the bearing his job required. In his Corps of Commissionaires uniform, he cut an impressive figure.

Charles Dawson with his memories.

Charles, now 79, recalls the World Cup Final of 1966 as a day of huge responsibility, but also as a day which passed off incident-free and with exactly the right result – 4-2 to England.

Part of Charles' success lay in distributing his men where they were needed most. Those with 'a bit of beef' were stationed in strategic locations. Their mere presence was enough. And for his success on the day and his skill on other occasions, Charles became something of a celebrity – the London cabbie who became the envy of football fans the length and the breadth of the country.

The World Cup Final doesn't particularly stand out in memory, he admits. But then again, he attended so many great games. He recalls that he turned up at Wembley at 11 o'clock on the day. His men turned up an hour later, three hours before kick-off. 'I was never nervous. I just accepted it as part of the job. But I was certainly excited. The atmosphere was absolutely fantastic and utterly trouble free. All you had to do was just speak to people and they would move to keep the gangways clear. Very often there would be little things, a bit of cheek back or they would push your cap up from behind, but not on that day.'

And so Charles was able to watch the game unhindered. He was also able to watch it with the huge advantage of complete freedom to go wherever he wanted. 'My job was to get around. I used to go on the perimeter and keep my eyes open. Sometimes I was up at the Press box making sure that there was no one there who shouldn't be. Sometimes I was right down by the touchline.'

And it's from that viewpoint that Charles can confirm that Geoff Hurst's controversial goal did in fact cross the line. 'I saw it all right. It was definitely a goal.' And when England scored, the stadium erupted. When the final whistle blew and the day was England's, it was just 'whoosh', Charles recalls. The West Germans were good, but the English were better.

Charles didn't get to know the players beyond a quick 'good luck' as they came up the tunnel onto the pitch. But on one occasion he got to know a couple of Scots fairly well. It was nine years later, the day England trounced the old enemy 5-1, prompting a Scots invasion.

One celebrated picture sees a row of policemen occupying the goal-mouth as the crowds surge forward. If you look carefully, you can see Charles dancing on the pitch with a Scottish fan. He confesses that it was a little bit of psychology. It hadn't been possible to keep the fans off the pitch, but Charles was at least doing his best to take the steam out of the situation.

Another picture from the same day sees Charles escorting another Scots fan from the pitch. The fan is struggling to keep his kilt on. Having laid the myth of Geoff Hurst's goal, Charles is able to nail another of life's imponderables. The Scots, it seems, do indeed wear something under their kilts. The picture, fortunately, offers all the proof you could ever wish for.

Less happy was the day Charles and The Rolling Stones went their separate ways.

Charles and his men were covering a series of Stones gigs at the Empire Pool Wembley. Several blokes nipped into seats temporarily vacated by a group of girls who had gone off for a cup of tea.

Charles' team tried to move the men on, at which point Mick Jagger is said to have shouted, '****off, sergeants. We don't need you.' Charles and his small army of ex-servicemen walked out. 'Just think', Charles was quoted in a national newspaper, 'We fought for the likes of him.'

No, Charles was most definitely not someone to be messed with …

[11 October 2001]

Bowling to Bradman Exciting?
Not really – it was just a Job

The greatest – that's the only way to describe the late Sir Donald Bradman. So says a man who had the good fortune never to have to bowl to him in earnest.

Former Sussex fast bowler Jack Nye, who now lives at Bosham, bowled to The Don in the nets in the early '30s, at the start of a career which saw Jack become the only county quickie to take a hundred wickets in the 1939 season. There seems little doubt that Jack would have gone on to play for England had the war not intervened. He was at his peak in that season, but the war robbed him of his chance to represent his country.

Jack, now 86, was born in Sussex, but spent much of his early life in Australia after his parents emigrated. Jack was 21 when he returned to Sussex with his mother and father. 'I came over to England with a chap called Alan Fairfax. He was a friend of Bradman's. They both played for Australia. I started at cricket school with him in London. I was one of the bowlers at the school through the winter.

'And I bowled against Bradman in the nets. He came down to the school to see how things were. Quite a lot of chaps wanted to bowl at him. This was about 1933. Some of us had our photographs taken with him.'

An exciting occasion?

'It didn't worry me. I was not all that much of a worshipper of cricketers. It was just a job.'

Jack first started playing for Sussex in about 1933 or 1934 and reached his best year in the summer of the year the Second World War erupted. After the war, he played a further season, but he found it tough going. 'I couldn't bowl on an empty stomach, and you could only get spam for lunch! I had got injured during the war, and I couldn't really go on. I kept pulling muscles. It wasn't really worth it. When you are in your 30s, you can't really start again. So I packed it in and went out to Africa to start a new life.'

Looking back, he can't recall his best bowling figures, but he can remember delivering the odd short one if the batters got 'nasty'.

A sad fact of his career, though, was that he was consistently over-bowled: 'I had to bowl too much. I would start bowling when the match started, and I would bowl right through until lunchtime. That was too

Fiery bowling from Jack Nye in his pomp as Sussex travel to Yorkshire.

*Sussex cricketer
Jack Nye.*

much. And then I would come back after lunch and bowl right through until tea. Sussex had no other bowlers in those days.'

His career brought him up against the greats, often with frustrating results. He recalls getting Wally Hammond out twice in a game at Worthing. Memories of Len Hutton aren't quite so happy. 'He was dropped off my first ball at Scarborough. He went on to get more than a hundred. Sutcliffe was the other one dropped first ball off me and went on to get a hundred. Those two batted all day for 200-300 runs.

'I should have had them both in the gully. They were hard catches, but they were catches. And the batsmen both went on to hit me all over the blooming ground.'

Hutton was undoubtedly a great: 'He was a very good type of batsman. He had a good eye and good timing. ... I remember playing against him once, and he got a big score. He got more than 200. And I remember he was almost making me bowl where he wanted it put!

'I also remember bowling to Compton and Edrich at Hove. It was an August Bank Holiday. I know I got Edrich out very easily. I don't remember what happened to Compton.'

*Jack Nye knocks
back the middle
stump and makes the
breakthrough for Sussex
against Yorkshire.*

Another great was Patsy Hendren against whom Jack bowled in Hendren's final game.

'He got more than a hundred before he got out, and I think he gave me his wicket. Very early on he had been given 'not out' and I think he knew he was out. So when he had got his hundred, he gave me his wicket.'

As for Bradman, yes, he was the greatest ever – but Jack remembers him very distinctly pre-bodyline and post-bodyline. 'I was in Australia at the time when bodyline was being played, and until then Bradman was absolutely untouchable. Then he had a bad time with bodyline.'

Jack later missed out on a game when Bradman played against Sussex. He remembers Bradman getting out very early on – much to the disappointment of a big crowd which then mostly went home.

[8 March 2001]

Rescued Papers recall a Cricketing Legend

Sussex and England cricketer Duleepsinhji will live on in his adopted county. The County Record Office in Chichester has acquired from India an entire archive charting some of the achievements of one of Sussex and England's greatest sportsmen.

The documents offer a fascinating insight into the man who still holds the record for the highest individual score ever made for Sussex.

His 333 also remains the highest innings ever played at Hove – more than 60 years after ill-health forced his early retirement from the game.

The papers owe their survival to Kushi Bahai Shah of Calcutta who rescued them from the ravages of heat and humidity. Through the good offices of a Sussex businessman and cricket enthusiast, the papers were brought to the attention of the County Record Office. After lengthy negotiations and with the help of the Duke of Richmond, president of Sussex County Cricket Club, and Roger Knight, the secretary of the Marylebone Cricket Club, the papers are now in Chichester.

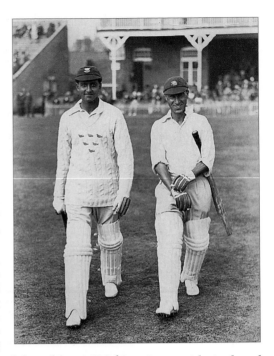

Sussex cricketing legend Duleepsinjhi (left) going out to open for his beloved county.

The collection consists of just over a hundred letters to Duleepsinhji written between 1923 and 1936, and a further 125 telegrams covering the same period, together with a letter and a telegram dated 1958 when he was Indian High Commissioner in Australia.

It also includes three scrapbooks of press cuttings and photographs telling the story of his career, two photograph albums — one personal, the other all cricket — and a box of photographs, most illustrating his cricketing career.

Among the letter writers are cricketers and characters of the standing of C.B. Fry, D.R. Jardine and Sir Pelham Warner. County archivist Richard Childs says: 'Some of the photographs in the collection are the standard Press photographs of the time, and there is unfortunately little about Duleepsinhji's private life. But the collection should form the basis for any future biography of one of Sussex and England's greatest sportsmen.'

Kumar Shri Duleepsinhji, nephew of the legendary Ranjitsinhji, made his first appearance in first-class cricket between leaving Cheltenham College in August 1923 and going up to Clare College, Cambridge, in October 1924. During this time he began a two-year residential qualification for Sussex, his uncle's county, and played a lot of club cricket in the county during the summer of 1924.

He first played for Sussex at Hove in June 1924 and continued to represent the county until he was forced to announce his premature retirement on grounds of ill-health in December 1933. He was given the captaincy of Sussex in 1931 and a year later led them to second place in the championship, a position they have never bettered.

Had he not collapsed in the pavilion at Taunton towards the end of the year and been forced to miss the remainder of the matches, Duleepsinhji, who was never on the losing side all season, might well have led Sussex to their first championship.

[24 August 1995]

Skills and Thrills of Sporting Glory

Above: *Charles Munro (right) with legendary boxer Randy Turpin, ex-world heavyweight champion, 1959.*

Below: *Charles Munro lands a punch on Brian White at Chichester Boys' Club in the 1950s.*

Charles Munro still revels in the excitement of Chichester's boxing glory days of the 1950s and early 1960s. For a decade and more, Chichester boasted a fine crop of highly talented boxers all set for great things.

Mr Munro, who now lives in Hinckley, Leicestershire, was just one of a number of enthusiastic boxers to emerge in Chichester 40 years ago.

Mr Munro was born in 1936 and came to live in Chichester with his family in the 1940s. It wasn't long before he was discovering his boxing skills. 'I was boxing right from when I was at the Lancastrian School right up until I was 18 plus. At the Lancastrian School there was a boxing club and Mr Barratt used to take the boxing there, and from there I joined the Chichester Boys Club where I continued boxing.

'From there I went to the Seal Club which was based at Earnley and which was run by a millionaire who had his own club in his back garden.

'We travelled to box up and down the South coast, Portsmouth, Southampton. I went to the Isle of Wight many times, and Brighton, all sorts of places. That was all in my teen years.'

He never suffered serious injury and insists now that these were experiences which 'made' his life. 'I made so many friends and it was good character-building stuff. All my aggression went into boxing. If it was not for boxing I might have gone the other way. It was a way of channelling aggression.'

His Boys Club days were the days when Bassil Shippam was running it, and Mr Munro was heartened at Easter when he returned to the club and discovered that boxing was still being taught there. 'In my day it was the in-thing. The great boxers of the time were Jack Hood and Johnny Weller. These were really big local lads. And there was Bernard Baker, Micky Flynn, Johnny White and Brian White. ... At the time Chichester had such a fantastic boxing club and you would never believe they won so many trophies.'

Mr Munro continued boxing in the army but gave up at around the age of 32. By then he had boxed in the British Army on the Rhine championships and had also boxed for Wales – not by virtue of being Welsh, but by virtue of being stationed there.

He became a coach and served as a PT instructor in the army. To this day he keeps up his interest by sponsoring his local club.

But his mind keeps coming back to Chichester's boxing heyday …
'I would love to meet my old foe Brian White again. I would love to
take him for two or three rounds. Rounds of drink that is, not boxing
rounds now!'

[20 June 1996]

Boxing Instructor's Legacy lives

Stefan Tucker used to be the kind of boy that other kids picked on – until
he joined Chichester Boys Club. By learning boxing he learned lessons
which have stood him in good stead ever since.

Stefan, now aged 41, remembers his five years with the club in the
late 1960s with great affection. 'I became a member of the Boys Club
when I was about 12, and the reason was that I was picked on at school.
There was no obvious reason. I would be pushed up against the rugby
post or whatever.'

But all that changed when his father introduced him to Boys Club
boxing instructor Arthur Preston, a policeman turned post office worker.
The lessons learned weren't without pain. Arthur's first trick was to
drop a heavy medicine ball on his stomach. 'The idea was to firm up the
muscles. The next time I was picked on, I stuck my shoulders back and
my stomach out and I took the blows just like that. They never tried it
again. They never bothered me after that.'

The discipline Stefan learned also involved control of temper, a vital
control for a successful boxer. Stefan, who was born and brought up in
Lavant and still lives there, recalls that Arthur would have the boys run
around the entire circuit of Chichester before they started sparring. 'It
must have been a good few miles when you take in all the little alleyways.
Arthur used to be there for three and a half hours of an evening, and he
really did a lot for us boys.'

It was a tough regime, but the result was a stamina which Stefan
remembers was unbelievable. 'He really brought that out of you. When
you felt that you had had enough, he would say "Oh no, you don't, you
keep going". He was pretty forceful but you really appreciate it looking
back.'

The young lads would wear 12oz boxing gloves, twice the weight that
boxers themselves use. 'You just look at the little weaklings we were,
wearing these big heavy gloves, but it used to build up your muscles.'

Stefan has long since given up boxing, and it was as a kind of tribute
to Arthur that Stefan didn't try to become an instructor himself. 'I don't
think anyone could take his place. He was understanding but firm. You
knew exactly where you stood with him. He was a friend to everybody.
You could tell him things you would probably never tell your father
– not that it came to it with me. But you could always tell him if you
were having an off day.'

Arthur has passed away now, but Stefan reckons that his legacy lives
on: 'He did a great deal for the community.'

[29 August 1996]

Chapter Eleven

SAINTS, SINNERS AND
ACTS OF GOD

Worst Blaze since the War

Shirley's in North Street was wrecked 20 years ago this month by a devastating blaze which threatened to engulf the whole heart of the city.

The Sainsbury's fire just before Christmas 1993 was a tragic spectacle, but the Shirley's fire was quite something else. Fire chiefs admitted that Sainsbury's, right on the city's edge and with a massive car park beside it, was a comparatively easy fire to fight and contain.

But Shirley's was a night-time blaze, right in the city centre, with people living nearby and a busy hotel just yards away. Paul White, who worked there, still remembers his 2.30a.m. wake-up call from his cashier: 'Mr White, the shop is on fire!' It was a wake-up call which effectively spelled the end of the line for one of Chichester's oldest family businesses.

Established in London in 1846 and brought to Chichester in 1955, the shop moved across the road within weeks of the fire but closed the following year. The blaze gutted the shop (now Dorothy Perkins), wrecking the Georgian facade and parts going back to the 14th century.

North Street was closed for days after, and on the night the blaze drew 120 firemen from West Sussex and Hampshire in 25 fire engines. The biggest Chichester blaze in living memory and certainly since the war, it caused damage put at a quarter of a million pounds and ominously threatened to spread.

The nearby *Dolphin and Anchor Hotel* was evacuated. Around 60 guests assembled in the main lounge before being led, some still in their night clothes, to the safety of the street. Wind from the south-west heightened fears for neighbouring buildings, and both Hendry's old shop which was undergoing renovation and the Southern Electricity Board on the other side were severely damaged. The Newell Centre in St Pancras became a centre for many families and their pets evacuated by police for safety.

How the Chichester Observer *reported the fire.*

Firemen wearing breathing apparatus entered the shop, but they were beaten back and all three storeys of the shop became a blackened shell destined for demolition. Meanwhile kitchen staff from the *Dolphin and Anchor* dished out hot soup in a Dunkirk spirit which returned to Chichester during the floods of January 1994.

Chichester had seen its worst blaze for many a year, and the changing face of the city's shopping streets had changed a little more.

[3 March 1994]

The Great Fire of Chichester

This year would have been the 230th anniversary of a remarkable Chichester printing business. Sadly, it went bust a couple of years ago. That it survived that long is a story in itself. A devastating fire could well have killed it off nearly four decades before its eventual demise.

Chichester Press Ltd was formed in 1949 but its roots can be traced back to 1768. In the end it fell just four years short of making it into its fourth century. But if it had not been for the determination of its employees and the energy of its bosses, its story could have ended in 1960. The company, dubbed the Chichester Phoenix, suffered a disastrous blaze which wrecked its premises, but then fought its way back and went on to survive for another 36 years.

The business, which had gone through a number of name changes, was already more than 150 years old when Messrs Owen-Jones and Avery turned it into Chichester Press just after the war. With a staff of 12, the company successfully sought London work, which Mr Owen-Jones would bring back to the Chichester Press premises in St Martin's Street.

And so it continued until the night of 26 March 1960 when a fire swept through the building, wrecking it in just half an hour.

A company publication, celebrating the 21st birthday of Chichester Press, recalls the physical and emotional devastation – and the determination which helped turn things round. 'Disaster – total loss by fire', it lamented. 'We wept. This, whilst obviously relieving some of the tension and shock, got us nowhere. The next day – the building still red hot and smouldering – found us all at work, getting communications going, finding out what we could about destroyed work in various ways, planning a new factory, buying new plant, and so on.'

The firm was in some sort of productive shape within days of the fire, operating from a small extension which had been saved, and five weeks later recorded the highest turn-over of any one month in its records. The company's new factory in Terminus Road was fully operational in the December, and soon turn-over was £15,000 up on the previous best.

The immediate problem, while the firemen were still playing their hoses on the steaming ruin in St Martin's Street, had been simply one of survival. It was decided that Mr Avery would look after all the production while Mr Owen-Jones would deal with the fire claim and oversee the building of the new factory. The company clawed its way back, going to ever greater heights in the 1960s and a turn-over of £4-£5 million.

Sadly 1996 proved more destructive than the fire. The printing firm went out of business. It had started in the 18th century; it had lived through the 19th; but it finally fell at the toe end of the 20th, with the 21st so tantalisingly close on the horizon.

[12 March 1998]

Top: *Dramatic scenes as Chichester's Sainsbury's goes up in smoke.*

Above: *Despite a heroic effort from the fire brigade, the store was devastated.*

Right: *Chichester's Sainsbury's superstore burnt long into the night, December 1993.*

The Day that West Dean made the
Front Page of the *Daily Mirror*

Presumably it's not often that West Dean makes the front page of the *Daily Mirror*. But that's just what happened on a grim day in 1934 – the day the church burned down. West Dean's royal connections ensured that the story was of national interest, as West Dean historian and life-long resident Eddie Glaister has discovered. He has been looking for pictures and details of the fire for the past 30 years and has come up with a range of images and cuttings.

Eddie can now confidently lay the ghosts of two particular myths. The fire was not in 1936. Nor was it in 1935. It was in 1934. And it was not caused by the electrics in the organ. There wasn't any electricity in the church, he says.

Eddie was born two years after the fire and has long been interested in the village and its history. The fire soon entered folklore even though the church was more or less rebuilt as it was. But it took quite some time before Eddie could nail the exact details.

The *Daily Mirror* certainly lapped up the story, with the headline 'Fire Ruins Historic Church Where King Edward Used To Worship'.

'Historic St Andrew's Church, at West Dean, Chichester, where King Edward frequently worshipped, was destroyed by fire yesterday', it proclaimed. 'At the height of the fire, the flames endangered West Dean Park, owned by Mr Edward James, who is abroad. King Edward paid frequent visits to West Dean Park when Mrs Willie James, the famous society beauty, reigned there as hostess.'

The alarm was given by a small boy who had been pumping the organ while a woman organist was practising. He raced to the vicarage and asked for help in putting the fire out 'as he had left his hat in the church'! The woman organist heard crackling noises coming from the organ and also rushed to the vicarage. The *Mirror* notes: 'The organ was a mass of flames and burnt like tinder. The blaze spread rapidly to the ancient beams and pews and to the vestry.'

Worse was to come. 'When the brigade arrived about 20 minutes later from Chichester, five miles away, they were powerless to fight the outbreak owing to the absence of water.' A small private supply was held in readiness. Four hours later the church was still smouldering.

The agent at West Dean Park, Mr Mackenzie, told the paper: 'We could see flames leaping through the roof, which collapsed in sections. Each time a piece fell, flames shot into the air.' He confirmed: 'The cause of the outbreak is unknown. The organ is not pumped electrically; in fact, there is no electric supply near it.'

So that ends the little myth about it being an electrical fire. But as Eddie notes, his cutting also creates another mystery and shows that times just don't change. On its front page, the *Mirror* trails a page-two story with the tantalising 'Woman Accuses A Vicar'. Now just what did she say?

In other respects, though, things have clearly moved on. Elsewhere the front page tells of the looming duel between two French MPs. 'Pistols', it notes, 'will settle a quarrel between two French Deputies, M Franklin-Bouillon, an Independent, and M Jean Goy, of the Radical Left

– that is if friends cannot talk them out of their anger.' Hitler, it seems, was at the root of their spat …

[27 September 2001]

Flood is Nothing New

'Our little stream', with its seasonal appearances and disappearances, is usually described as intermittent. But as torrential rain brought New Year flood chaos to much of the Chichester area, the River Lavant was transformed almost beyond recognition into a raging, gushing mass of water. The modest river, best known for the number of times it goes out of sight in its brief journey to the sea, was suddenly flowing with colossal force, leaving few people unaware of its presence.

The rain-swollen River Lavant burst its banks in Chichester for the first time in half a century, and the immediate effect was flooding, with huge quantities of water pouring into The Hornet and New Park Road. The less immediate effect was that a flood of historians went scurrying through their records to find out when things were last as bad as this.

Ken Newbury, an expert on the river with a book on the subject to his credit, admitted: 'I should think it is as bad as it ever has been in living memory.' In the introduction to his book, he says he has always delighted in the fact that Chichester possesses a river, however small and elusive. The result of that delight was *The River Lavant*, published by Phillimore in 1987, a volume which recalls other occasions when Chichester's poodle became a rottweiler.

A very wet Chichester … St Pancras, looking towards Westhampnett, in the 1870s.

Floods are nothing new: Chichester's New Park Road in the 1930s.

James Spershott, born in 1710, whose memoirs are an important document in Chichester's history, wrote in 1771: 'The new bridge built over the Lavant without the East Gate before which the water lies open, spread wide and, when the springs were high, flow'd [ie flooded] from within a few yards of East Gate into The Hornet as far as the Poor House, and was so deep in the current that I have seen it above the beds of the waggons.

'There was then only a narrow bridge of two stone arches from The Hornet to the Pancras for horse and foot people.'

After Spershott's death in 1789, the notebook containing his memoirs is continued in a different hand for the years 1797 to 1809. This last year includes the following note: 'February. The water of the Lavant run all round the city occasioned by its overflowing its banks which flowed the lower rooms in St Pancras and The Hornet.

'Run rapidly into the lane to St Michael's Fair Field [New Park Road], so into the Lighten [The Litten] and flowed the Bishop's Garden Field [the present Jubilee Gardens] and found its way round to the North Gate as in the year 1763, which may be e'pected once in 50 years.'

More flooding came in December 1960, as the *Chichester Observer* noted: 'Wearing rubber boots and armed with buckets and mops, shopkeepers and householders in St Pancras have been anxiously watching the water level in the River Lavant.

'Many have been hit hard by the flow which burst from the Lavant after the gale, rising above sandbagging and pouring into the cellars, kitchens, shops and showrooms. ... Between 25 and 30 workmen from the West Sussex River Board and the City Council piled sandbags in a wall beside the Lavant and against doors, front gates, and cellar grids in an attempt to keep houses dry.

'For the first time in memory, it poured over the footbridge from St Pancras to Green Lane, and workmen had to build a wooden plank bridge across it on sandbags.'

[13 January 1994]

142

Camaraderie 'in the Bunker'

West Sussex county information officer Jane Robinson remembers most the sheer camaraderie of life in the 'bunker' during Chichester's flood emergency. The command centre for controlling the Chichester flood operations – exactly one year ago – was a place of long hours and intense pressure.

But through it all, teamwork and a sense of humour kept the workers going in the dark days of January 1994. 'There was this incredible camaraderie', Mrs Robinson recalls. 'We had a laugh and we managed to have some fun.' The bunker operated for about ten days, and some of the days meant up to 17 hours on duty. 'It tended to be pressure all the time, although there were lulls in the middle of the night. When there was pressure you were awake, but when it would go quiet, you would start to nod.'

Looking back, she reckons at no moment did they fear the situation was getting out of control. 'The important thing was that everybody was acting as a team. We were all together, all up-to-date. I didn't feel it was running away from us.' With Martin O'Neill, Mrs Robinson's role was to field questions from an ever-eager media. 'The vast majority of the media behaved in an exemplary fashion. There was a minority that wanted sensationalism, making out that Chichester was cut off. These people made life difficult for the traders.'

Floodwaters besieged Chichester in the early weeks of 1994.

Taking the dogs for a swim in Lavant. As the sign says, no footway ...

But overall, the Press responded positively and responsibly to the emergency. 'It's amazing to think that it's a year ago now. So much has happened since, what with the Local Government Review this year, that it is dimmer perhaps in memory now. ... But the point is we need to be prepared, and we are prepared. The county has emergency plans and we swing into action immediately we get something like this. ... It went to prove that the plans that we had were essentially OK when the real emergency happened. It was just a matter of dotting the i's and crossing the t's.'

Since then, a floods working party has investigated the response, and recommendations for fine-tuning have emerged.

The flood seemed like the kind of thing which couldn't happen twice, but Mrs Robinson points out that the 1987 hurricane was supposed to have been a once-in-a-200-year-event. It happened again three years later. 'You never know with emergencies when they are going to happen. You never discount anything like this happening. The important thing is to have plans and to be able to swing into action as a team. ... We can certainly do that.'

[5 January 1995]

What they said ...

A year ago this week, Chichester was in the grip of its worst flooding for more than a century. The *Chichester Observer* channelled a flood of words in response. Here we reproduce a few floodbites.

The floods

Fire brigade spokesman: 'It has been just flood, flood, flood. Bosham, Wittering, just about everyone has been affected. It has been the whole of the county.'

Farmer Gary Scott: 'Out of the blue a torrent of water came rushing in.'

Singleton landlady Ruth O'Connell: 'Water is coming up through the floor. We have run out of sandbags.'

The misery

Tricia Gick, of Bosham Hoe: 'Before I knew where I was, the car was up to the headlights in water. I didn't know what to do. My instinct was to put my foot down and go through it. But in fact the problem was solved for me when the engine cut out.'

Singleton resident Lillian Mills: 'I am really frightened. There is a lake all around me, and I am just about marooned in my house. I have never seen the river so high.'

The trauma

Fishbourne resident David Thair: 'I was on my bike's lowest gear to keep going. The water was knee-deep in Fishbourne Road East.'

Undertaker Kevin Holland after funerals were cancelled at Chichester crematorium: 'The families have been very sympathetic to us, knowing that it is an act of God rather than anyone's fault.'

It's not often that you need a dinghy in Stoughton ...

The traders

Anon: 'It's like being on a sinking ship.'

John Dent, of Chichester Bookshop: 'Yesterday we had three sales and on Monday two. Trade is really suffering.'

The heroes

Geoff Georgiades, Hornet cafe owner: 'Our police and our firemen are like public relations officers. They come in smiling. There is a great spirit of all being in it together'.

Flood victim Maureen Davis-Poynter, of Chichester: 'The firemen have been absolutely incredible and we cannot praise them highly enough. They have been cheerful, considerate, courteous and caring.'

A surreal sight on what should have been a busy road.

Flood spirit

Roadworker Paul Adams, of Bognor Regis: 'The job had to be done and you just had to go on and do it. The British are good at this sort of thing. They thrive in a panic situation. We noticed that everyone was cool, calm and collected.'

The big effort

Steve Lawlor, catering manager for County Hall: 'It was really a case of in at the deep end. In the last week, we have served around a thousand hot meals a day.'

County Hall chief cook Sally Drake: 'One soldier told me we were feeding him better than his own mum!'

The reasons

The Revd Richard Griffiths, rector of St Pancras: 'It is clear that when you put a lot of buildings on what people call a flood plain, all the water that used to flood there must still go somewhere.'

Teresa Cash, National Rivers Authority spokeswoman: 'The cause is exceptionally atrocious weather conditions, a very wet autumn culminating in a deluge just after Christmas. We have already had double the average rainfall for January at this stage, and we are only half way through the month.'

[5 January 1995]

146

Antique Dealer accused of stealing Crown Jewels

Chichester historian Ken Green admits he has come to a halt in his researches into the life of one of the city's shadowier figures. Mr Green, following a request from Irish historian Sean Hannafin, is trying to trace any information about Francis Richard Shackleton who lived and died in Chichester in the early 1940s.

Francis was the younger brother of Sir Ernest Shackleton, the polar explorer who was a junior officer on Scott's 1901 expedition to Antarctica and who himself died leading an expedition to South Georgia in 1922.

But so far Mr Green's endeavours have failed to uncover much about Francis. What is known for sure is that, before he came to Chichester, Francis was appointed to the Irish Office of Arms as Cork Herald, based in Dublin Castle. It was an office responsible for the custody of the Irish Crown Jewels, and it was here that Francis' misfortunes began.

In 1907 the jewels – or, more correctly, The Insignia Of The Illustrious Order Of St Patrick, an order of 16 knights, instituted by King George III in 1783 – were stolen from the castle. 'Shackleton was the prime suspect, but was never convicted of the crime', Mr Green says.

'In later years he served a jail sentence in England for company fraud. Such was the disgrace to the family that he was made to change his name to Mellor.' Mr Green's researches reveal that it was as F.R.S. Mellor that Shackleton came to Chichester in about 1934 where he managed to lease The Crypt in South Street from the Cathedral authorities and set up in business as an antique dealer and genealogist.

'No doubt using the skills he obtained during his time as Cork Herald he also offered his services as a painter of coats of arms. He lived in another church property, No 2 St Faith's, within the Cathedral Close.'

He died in poverty on 24 June 1941 in St Richard's Hospital and was buried in a grave in Chichester cemetery which was dug for three burials. In April 1953 his sister Amy Vibert Shackleton joined him in the plot, but the third grave has not been taken up.

From local directories Mr Green has found that another sister, Miss G Mellor, took over the business in about 1942 and later it was owned by Amy Shackleton until it closed. Both women also lived at No 2 St Faith's.

In his 1978 book *Chichester: The Valiant Years*, Bernard Price showed a picture of The Crypt as an antique furniture shop and recollected the Misses Shackleton who ran it. But there the trail stops ...

[25 January 1996]

Shocking Mystery has never been solved

It was one of the great crime sensations of 1924. It was also one of the most heart-breaking. Little Vera Hoad loved music, and Monday was music day. At 6.30p.m. she left her lesson and headed home to St Pancras. She was not seen alive again. Three days later she was found at Graylingwell, a layer of snow her only shroud. She had been strangled and violated.

The discovery rocked Chichester, and all manner of rumour did the rounds as police knocked on door after door in a vain effort to find a clue to the killer. A piece of cloth, perhaps from the killer's clothes, sent shivers through the city.

Washing hanging in the back garden became a rare sight. No one dared offer anyone the chance to find a ripped garment. Two and two would have made five, six or seven in the climate of fear and suspicion. But time passed and the horror subsided. Police inquiries continued, but little came to light. Scotland Yard was at its most diligent, but the person guilty of the atrocious crime was never traced. As *The News Of The World* wrote nine years later when Vera's father committed suicide, the tragedy passed into the pigeon holes of murders unsolved.

Now, for the first time, a Chichester woman has broken her 70-year silence. Little Vera was her friend, a bright young girl she loved to play with. Her death has stayed with her ever since. Vera Hoad was a 'bonny child of happy disposition and fair bobbed hair', the *Chichester Observer* wrote when her strangled body was found at Graylingwell.

Seventy years later, that's just how her one-time friend still remembers her. 'She was a very bright little girl, always laughing, always joking, riding around on her bike.'

Now 80, Vera's friend asks for her name not to be revealed, but she talks freely of the friend she lost to an unknown killer on 25 February 1924.

Her memories are just as fresh now as they ever were. She and Vera used to meet before and after school, and the day 11-year-old Vera disappeared was no different.

'We were coming down the road and she was just going off for a music lesson. She said "Cheerio, see you tomorrow". I never saw her again.

'She was missing, I don't know, three or four days, and all these rumours were going round. My mother wouldn't let me know what was being said, but I flapped my ears.

'And then Vera was found at Graylingwell by a deaf and dumb patient. This dummy, as people used to call them, tried to get people to understand that he wanted someone to go with him, and it took him some time. ... When they got there, they found her. She was absolutely frozen solid on to the ground. They had to get a blow torch to release her.'

Vera Hoad, a 'bonny child', who died a tragic death.

THE VERA HOAD MURDER.

STORY AT THE INQUEST.

NO FURTHER LIGHT ON MYSTERY.

The resumed inquest on Monday on the 11 and a half year old Chichester schoolgirl, Vera Hoad, who was found murdered in a field on the Graylingwell Mental Hospital farm on February 28th, brought to light very few facts beyond those with which the public were already acquainted, and indicated that the tragedy is up to the present, almost as big a mystery as ever.

The only evidence submitted as to Vera having been last seen alive was that of Mrs. Rickard, the mother of the girl's music teacher, who saw her leave her house in St. Paul's road on the night of her disappearance at 6.40 p.m.

see her to the end of the street.

The Foreman: Did she appear to be in a hurry to leave.

Witness: No; not at all.

A juryman: Did you notice anyone else about at the time she was leaving.

Mrs. Rickard: No.

Last to See her Alive.

The Coroner: This is the last person who saw poor Vera alive that we know of ?

Mr. Dell: Yes, sir.

William Arthur Peacock, estate bailiff to the Graylingwell Hospital, then gave his evidence, relating to the discovery of

No effort could bring the killer to book ... how the Chichester Observer *reported the inquest.*

THE NEWS OF THE WORLD

MR. HOAD AND HIS DAUGHTER VERA.

Vera Hoad's murder was never solved. Nine years later her father committed suicide.

Only now, a lifetime later, has the friend learned that Vera was strangled. The precise details of Vera's dreadful fate were kept from her. 'All I know was that we had the detectives coming round asking all these questions. ... They were going around with a piece of a shirt, a man's shirt. People were frightened to hang their washing out after that if they had a patch on their shirts. There was a terrific to-do about the whole thing. ... Those days people had little to interest them so something like this was really big news. Nowadays people get murdered, and it is just one a week. ... The detectives were asking me if Vera played with boys, if I could say whether she had said anything. I couldn't think whether or not she had. I was just too terrified. I hid behind my mother.'

She added: 'I have been looking through a book on murders in Sussex, and I looked all through it and I couldn't see any reference to this case, but it was a big noise at the time.

'She was buried in Westhampnett cemetery, now Portfield. It was just a simple grave with a headstone. I tried to find it the last time I was in the cemetery, and I couldn't actually find it. I know the area. I'm sure I could find it if I tried again some time.'

The woman didn't attend the burial and didn't even know it was on – again part of the protective cloak spread around her by her family. But afterwards she became good friends with Vera's mother, a deeply religious woman who turned to séances in an attempt to solve the crime. A medium told her that it was someone called Jack who committed the murder, but Mrs Hoad knew no one of that name, and there it remained – a story that has haunted Vera's school friend ever since.

'I remember Vera so well. She was such a bright and happy sort of girl. I often used to wonder what she would have become if she had lived. I can see her now.'

[11 August 1994]

Crowds came out – whatever the Occasion

Jeanne Whitbourn chanced on a recent copy of the *Chichester Observer*. It contained a photograph of the crowds which gathered in the city on the day Elizabeth was proclaimed Queen. It was a picture which brought the memories flooding back.

Jeanne lives in Stroud, but her son, who lives in Hampshire, bought her the *Chichester Observer*. In it she found a welcome reminder of the day she saw history in the making. Half a century ago, Jeanne was a trainee teacher at Bishop Otter teacher training college. 'I had suffered a particularly bad bout of flu and had been sent home to convalesce,' she explained.

'On returning to college, I had walked up South Street from the station and came upon this ceremony at the Cross, quite unaware as to what was happening as I had been ill.

'Later I realised that I had witnessed a rare historical event – the proclamation of the new Queen.'

In some ways, it all seems a long time ago. In some ways, it doesn't. But these were certainly happy days 'I loved Chichester' she says. 'It was two years that I had there. I suppose I feel about it the way most people do about places where they were students. You are on your own and you are having a good time ... My husband and I were both born and bred in Sussex. We have always loved Sussex, and we always love going back there.

Chichester has grown so much since I was at college there, but it was just such a nice compact little city. It was a Church of England college then, and we had a lot of connections with the Cathedral. There were lots of occasions when we would have to go there for different purposes.'

All in all, the city gave her a good start in her teaching career. She went on to teach at places including Horsham, Hove and Worthing before moving to Gloucestershire. But Chichester has always retained a special place in her affections. After all, it was in Chichester that she entered the new Elizabethan era.

[30 May 2002]

Crowds gather in Chichester for the proclamation of Queen Elizabeth II on 8 February 1952.

Piano took a Bit of a Beating on Jubilee Day

The poor old piano was the victim when the residents of Chichester's Cambrai Avenue got together to celebrate the Queen's Silver Jubilee. The weather was dire a quarter of a century ago, but the rain didn't dampen the spirits of the people of Cambrai Avenue. Despite the rain, Mr and Mrs Williams brought their piano out of the house and put it by the kerb.

Queen Elizabeth II was a visitor to Chichester on 30 July 1956.

'There was a stool there so that another person and I played, and we were able to have a sing-song in the rain,' recalls Ken Newbury, who was among the party-goers. 'I think we did do Singing In The Rain!'

The piano's owners had been teaching their children to play and had stuck little labels on the notes to help them identify them. In the rain, these labels came loose and weren't exactly conducive to ease of playing. 'It was all rather glissando', Ken recalls. But further indignities were in store for the piano. Ken admits that it probably wasn't in the best of shape to start with, but worse was to follow. The Mayor of Chichester was touring the city dropping in at various parties and doubtless having a cup of tea at each. And then he came to Cambrai Avenue. He perched his cup on the top of the piano. Sadly, it didn't stay there long, and the upturned tea tumbled into the piano's most intimate workings. 'Tea For Two would have been the most appropriate song at that point', Ken recalls.

[30 May 2002]

It's Quality, not Quantity that Counts

Dennis Burgess reserved a hard look and a quick answer for the silk-hankied West End ladies who would swan in and ask 'How many boys do you have in your Chichester Boys Club?' 'I would ask them "Why? Surely the question is what do you do with the members. Would it really impress you more if I had 50, 500 or 5,000?"'

In Dennis' view quality was everything when it came to youth work, and when he stepped down as leader in 1980 he deplored the increasing obsession with numbers. 'I used to estimate what I called saturation point!' Dennis recalls. 'When you have got enough members to cover all the activities you have got, you don't want any surplus. If you have got 20 or 30 surplus, they are going to go around creating problems. ... When I left I said I was sorry that numbers had become the name of the game and not quality.'

It was this quest for quality which added an extra dimension to Dennis' many years in youth work. 'In the past the emphasis was on a three-fold programme – physical, educational and social,' Dennis recalls. 'But I always figured that that programme pandered to the selfishness of youngsters, the kind of attitude that says "why can't we have a minibus?"'

'My attitude was to add a fourth side to the programme which I didn't label Christian because we had all sorts as members, but which I used to call on-going community service.'

Dennis, aged 79, of Lime Close, put it into practice in his pre-Chichester days in Stratford, London, when he organised teams of girls to help out at a hospital and teams of boys to help out at an old people's home. 'When we came down to Chichester, I had a look around. What I was used to was working in a down-beaten area with lots of unemployment and semi-bombed areas not yet rebuilt. Down in Chichester, it was much more conservative.' Dennis directed his community projects towards the elderly, collecting wood for distribution among pensioners unable to get out and get it for themselves. Dennis also came up with his 'flashing red light scheme' in which the Boys Club provided specially-constructed boxes for elderly people to put into their windows. The boxes contained a light which would flash when activated by a switch at the end of a cable. Police, post office and milkmen were informed that a flashing light meant the occupant was in trouble or distress.

Dennis recalls that the installation wasn't always straightforward. One elderly woman was happy for the box to go in her front window, but she wanted the switch hanging from her budgie cage in the back room – a feat which required a fair amount of drilling and cabling. On another occasion, Boys Club members found themselves hacking through thick ice in a particularly bitter winter to make the ground passable. 'We had to really chop it up in squares. It was quite some tough work.'

[1 August 1996]

Hospital had no Equipment – and only one Nurse

Sylvia Dadswell can claim the distinction of having been the first nurse at Chichester's St Richard's Hospital – and for two days she was its only nurse.

Nurses in the ward, at the Royal West Sussex Hospital, Chichester, in 1954.

Mrs Dadswell – then Miss Halfacree – came to West Sussex after her nursing training at Barnet General Hospital. She responded to an advertisement which offered nurses the chance to work at a new hospital between the Downs and the sea. She arrived to find a shell. And she couldn't have arrived at a more solemnly momentous moment – September 1939.

Christmas at
St Richard's Hospital,
Chichester, in 1955.

Mrs Dadswell, now 81 and living in Duncton, was faced with a hospital with no equipment, and this just two days after war was declared 'From the word go we were setting the hospital up,' she recalls 'There was a room off the landing packed to the ceiling with a great mound of blankets. I can smell them now. And there were piles of bedsteads.

'The hospital wasn't ready. There was no staff. I was the first nurse there, and for 48 hours I was the only nurse there.' But the new hospital was soon into its stride. It had to be. The world was at war. 'The Germans used to try to bomb Portsmouth, and when they bombed Portsmouth all the lights at St Richard's went out. 'We had lots of people evacuated to us. On one occasion they evacuated the Gosport War Memorial Hospital which was full of children. They arrived at St Richard's in the middle of the night, and it was chaos. ... The lights had gone out, and the children arrived without any preparation. And then later that night terribly-worried mums arrived. It was an experience to say the least.'

Another effect of the bombing was that the laundry would be put out of action, which put paid to nappies and the like. 'So a lot of the time we were very short of linen,' Mrs Dadswell remembers. 'And then on one occasion we had a hut completely full of wounded German airmen. They were all very young men, some with terrible injuries. We had soldiers with rifles outside the door and all sorts of security.

'But I don't think there would have been any trouble. They were worried to death and wanted to be back home with their girlfriends and wives and families. They were just ordinary nice young men. We looked after them like they were our brothers.' Mrs Dadswell left St Richard's after a couple of years to have a family of her own. With her husband, a policeman, she moved to Rake, near Petersfield, where she was later to become the first nurse for what was to become the Leonard Cheshire Foundation.

But in 1953 she returned to St Richard's where she remained until her retirement in 1978. It was a different hospital she found – bigger and with better supplies including sterilised bottles of blood. Even then, though, the operating theatre wasn't built. 'But I loved every minute of it. I love every stone of the place.'

[16 July, 1998]

Molly – and a life of Building Fences to protect Others

There was a saying in the profession: 'It's better to build the fence at the top of the cliffs rather than maintain an ambulance at the bottom.' And it's a saying which sums up Molly Corbally's many years as a health visitor in the Midlands in the days after the Second World War,

Molly, who trained as a nurse at the old Royal West Sussex Hospital in Chichester, says the task was a case of health visiting minus the social workers. Voluntary bodies and charities gave first-class support, but Molly and her fellow health visitors were basically alone, solely in charge of the general health of the families in their care.

It was a system where the responsibilities were clear. As Molly recalls: 'It's not like today where social workers think that health visitors are making a visit and the health visitors think that the social workers are making the visit, and the visit doesn't get done.

'That wouldn't have happened in my day. There was only one person that could have made the visit, and that visit was made.' And that was a big part of the satisfaction in a truly satisfying job, Molly recalls. It was a job in which she was able to make a difference. By erecting 'the fences on the top of the cliffs', she was actively preventing illness. 'It was a question of seeing the children from the word go and making sure they had a good start in life, properly fed and cared for and given all the necessary inoculations. In my time TB was eliminated. When I started it was rampant.'

A key enemy was ignorance. For many families, the bath was nothing more than a convenient place in which to store the coal. Cleanliness went out the window. Even with the better-off families who employed nannies, there was still a job to be done. 'I used to find that some of the nannies were thrilled to bits to have someone they could ask questions. They didn't want their employers to know that they didn't know it all.'

The advent of health workers transformed doctors' surgeries. Molly remembers one case where a doctor prescribed a child an enema to treat its constipation. Molly saw that the best approach was simply to change the child's diet. Again, she was the 'fence' preventing the child tumbling to the 'ambulance' below. It was rewarding work and she was given the very best possible foundation by the Royal West Sussex where Molly, now 88, started her training in 1930.

'I think the training we had would compare very favourably with any hospital today. It was an exceedingly efficient hospital. It was small and we were very very well trained. … The advantage of it being a little hospital was that you did everything. In London there are so many specialist hospitals. When you got to a provincial town like Chichester, you would experience all sorts of conditions. Nursing is always hard work. You came off from a night duty and you might have to report for a lecture at 10 am. Your lectures were tied in with your work. It was much tougher in those days.' But there were compensations. The trainee nurses in Chichester 'lived in', they were fed, and they had no expenses at all. Instead of pay, they had pocket money – £18 a year. 'It went a bit further than it would do today, but it didn't go very far. If you broke a thermometer or something, that was a few pence out of your own money!'

[1 November 2001]

Déjà vu for New Park Campaigners

There's more than a touch of déjà vu about the campaign to save Chichester's New Park Centre from possible demolition. Centre honorary president George Appleby has been there before. He's hoping this time round the same argument will prevail: the centre is a hugely precious value-for-money community asset.

Mr Appleby speaks with the knowledge of a founding father. Twenty five years ago this year, he was among those who successfully persuaded the district council that the former school was viable as a full-time community centre. 'The school was put up after the 1872 or 1874 Education Act which required local authorities to provide elementary education for all the local children', Mr Appleby explains. 'This big Act put the responsibility on the local education authorities. They set up two schools there – the boys' school and the girls' school.

'When I came down to Chichester in 1970, the girls' school had been knocked down and turned into car parking. The boys' school remained, but the boys had moved out some time in the late '50s or early '60s to new premises in Orchard Street.

'The old school had been sitting there. It was a useful building, and the city council, who owned it at the time, rented it out to a number of local clubs and societies. My son went to the playgroup that ran at the centre.

George Appleby (right) and friends give the New Park Centre a facelift in 1974.

'And then I heard with dismay that the playgroup was going to stop because the district council was going to close the old building. They decided that it was unsafe.

'The district council had inherited it from the city council. They had a look at it and decided that it was in poor repair. The chief executive Peter Lomas had a walk around it, switched on the light and got an electric shock. They concluded it just wasn't safe. ... The valley gutters between the roofs were a century old. The lead was worn out so the walls were damp and the damp had got into the wiring. They said, 'That's it then, this is unsafe, we will knock it down'.

'There was also at the time the great Chichester redevelopment dispute. They were talking about the great reorganisation of Chichester, making the centre traffic free. To enable this, they wanted to put a dual carriageway ring road right the way around the centre – like the Avenue de Chartres but right the way round.

'Looking at the old New Park Road school they thought, "If we knock the old building down, we could dual New Park Road and that will pick up the dual at Franklin Place".

'But the Chichester Society didn't want to see the school knocked down, and they particularly didn't want the dual carriageway. When one of the new district councillors called a public meeting to discuss the future of the old school, I went along as a parent and as a representative of the Chichester Society. ... At this meeting we had a splendid young architect who said that the building might be electrically unsafe, but structurally it was as sound as a bell. The electricity angle could be dealt with by renewing the valley guttering and rewiring it.

'At the meeting a steering committee was formed to save the building. It was born of the five original clubs using it – the Chichester Players, Chichester Judo, the New Park playgroup, the youth theatre group and the Chichester Model Aeroplane Society. I came out of that meeting finding myself chairman of the steering committee. ... The other three that joined in and gave us some real muscle were the Chichester Society, the Civic Society and the Environmental Trust.

'We got in touch with as many members of the district council as we could in advance of the council meeting that would confirm or not the sub-committee's recommendation to demolish. The big one was this full council meeting, and we nobbled as many people as we could.

'It was debated at great length, and I think we would have lost the case had the chairman of the council not said "We can't go on talking about this any longer, let's hand it over to a sub-committee." If it had been voted on, it would have been demolished. In the event, the sub-committee met with the steering committee and they gave us six months to carry out the first-line repairs to make the building safe. That meant raising £7,000.'

The *Chichester Observer* reported the campaign under the headline 'And Now The Big Facelift'.

'I think the council were trying to see whether we were just sentimental anti-demolitionists or whether we were serious enough to get stuck in. That was the challenge.' And it was a challenge fully realised. The deadline was met, the former school became a community centre and the range of groups using it rapidly expanded. Old classrooms were knocked together to form a gymnasium. Two classrooms were knocked together to form a theatre for the Chichester Players. Since then, the theatre has become home to Chichester's arts cinema. 'Recently the old school dining rooms next door were handed over. Half of that is used as a jazz studio. Jazz is our biggest user.'

The quarter of a century since the campaign was won has seen the centre established as a major community asset – precisely the argument Mr Appleby and his colleagues used ten years or so ago when the prospect of demolition reared its head once more. And it's precisely the argument they are using now that demolition is again on the cards as part of district council redevelopment plans for the area. 'I am reasonably confident we will win,' Mr Appleby said. Once again, the arguments will be pitched along the lines of cost and the great self-help tradition. Having saved it twice, Mr Appleby and his supporters aren't going to let it go now.

[3 June 1999]

Bishop Bell: an Inspirational Leader

A charismatic church leader of inspirational devotion and humanity, Bishop Bell of Chichester (1883-1958) left a lasting legacy through his teaching and through his example.

Bishop Bell is seen here at the laying of the first bricks for Chichester's Whyke Housing Estate.

But he wasn't necessarily a modest man. 'He didn't go around wringing his hands and saying "poor unworthy me" recalls Roy Porter, who spent two years as Bell's domestic chaplain in the late 1940s. 'The Bishop had a very keen sense of his talents and merits!' Talents and merits which were considerable.

Bell was one of the few dignitaries in the Anglican church to enjoy worldwide fame, a point made in *Bell Of Chichester*, the 17th in the series of Otter Memorial Papers published by University College Chichester. Bell's work for the World Council of Churches and his stand in the House of Lords on 9 February 1944 against the policy of obliteration bombing of Germany are regarded as defining features of his episcopate. But his work went further still. He rediscovered the Church as a patron of the arts, organised centres for the reception of refugees from Nazi Germany and welcomed Mahatma Gandhi to The Palace at Chichester, though not himself a pacifist. Roy Porter, who went on to become professor of theology at Exeter University, was among those to contribute an essay on his former boss. Professor Porter remembers Bishop Bell with great affection and with great respect.

Professor Porter was Bell's domestic chaplain in a very literal sense. 'I lived in the Bishop's Palace', Professor Porter recalls. 'In those days, the Tudor Room was the dining room, and I had all my meals with the Bishop and Mrs Bell. They were extremely hospitable people. There was hardly a day that went by without there being somebody to lunch or dinner.

'He was a very special man indeed. He was also extremely hard-working. His whole life was devoted to being Bishop of Chichester. Anything he read or saw he tried to draw into his episcopal ministry. If he read a book by somebody, he would be trying to get them to come and give a talk in Chichester.

'He really was at work all day. I always remember after I had been here a couple of months, I said to him "I know you can do this, but I really can't. I really must have a day off" He was very kind and said yes, but it never really happened!'

Looking back, Professor Porter remembers straightforwardness as Bell's principal quality.

'He could not abide shifty, deceitful people. Some of the clergy tried to pull the wool over his eyes over things, and that really irritated him. He very rarely lost his temper, but when he did it was memorable.'

Professor Porter also remembers him as a man of very deep Christian faith – a faith of a kind which might well be considered traditional today but which would not have been considered so then. 'I mean particularly in his ecumenical interests which made him seem radical back then but wouldn't seem so now,' Professor Porter recalls. 'But they sprang from a very clear idea that he wanted to reconcile and bring into one all Christian people.

'And it was that that was behind his work in trying to reconcile Germany with England after the war. He wanted to unite all believers and all people of good will.'

Was his speech to the House of Lords an act of courage? Bell wouldn't have seen it that way, Professor Porter believes: 'It was just something that he felt very deeply because he was thinking of the ordinary German people, not the Nazis and the generals, but the ordinary German people who suffered so terribly.'

Also remembering Bell with affection at the book launch was his former secretary Mary Joice (née Balmer) who worked for him from 1941 more or less until his death. The dates mean that she was very much on the receiving end for the backlash which greeted Bell's House of Lords speech) 'People used to ring up', she remembers. 'He didn't know. I took the calls, and they would call him every name under the sun. But I would stand up for him.' As for Bell, he never had the remotest shadow of a doubt that his was the right stance to take.

'He was a wonderful man,' recalls Mrs Joice who is in her 90th year, 'He was very good-tempered and very hard-working. He would never go to bed on the day he got up!

'I remember once Penguin Books were going to produce a book about something to do with the church, and they said they could only produce it if it could be written in six weeks. Bishop Bell said he would do it.

'He and I used to meet every evening as extra time and we would plough through this book. He was wonderful in the way that he got it done.'

[4 March 2004]

The Day Gandhi Popped in on Chichester and Bognor

Well, here's one of the more unlikely photos you'll ever see – Mahatma Gandhi making a social call in Bognor Regis. The occasion was an autumn weekend in 1931 when the Indian leader came to stay with Bishop Bell in Chichester. It was an occasion which threw up a few myths which still do the rounds today. Did the Mahatma really bring a goat with him and tether it on the Cathedral Green? Does anyone know?

It's one of those stories that really ought to be true. More certain is the fact that he brought his spinning wheel with him. As the *Chichester Observer* reported at the time, he always did. But it has to be said that the *Chichester Observer* isn't much help to anyone wishing to find out a little bit more.

Admittedly the Mahatma wasn't quite then the icon he is now, but even so, the *Observer's* four-paragraph account, tucked away on page two, probably didn't do the great man justice. Gandhi himself would probably have been serenely unperturbed by the fact that he failed to knock the Melody Makers Dance Band live at the Pavilion Garden, Bognor, off the

Gandhi leaving 'The Lawn', Campbell Road, Bognor Regis, on Sunday 11 October 1931. He is accompanied by his friend C.P. Scott, the former editor of the Manchester Guardian.

front page. And he probably wouldn't have minded the fact that he was further back in the paper than the announcement from Messrs Lindsey and Son of Portsmouth that they had successfully devised a 'NEW TYPE of ELASTIC TRUSS which is soft and comfortable and will control your rupture at all times and under all conditions'.

But it does seem strange that the Mahatma's visit occupied half the space given to the inquest into the death of a Felpham housewife, a third of the space given to the sudden death of a Chichester trader and considerably less space than was given to the horse-racing at Fontwell. But then this was clearly a different world – a world in which even the fanfare the Mahatma received in Chichester was intended for something else entirely.

As the *Chichester Observer* wrote: 'A large crowd was near the Cross, Chichester, on Saturday evening, eagerly waiting to catch a glimpse of Mr Gandhi who came for a quiet weekend with the Bishop of Chichester and Mrs Bell.

'They were able to get a good view of him for the car had to slow down just before it got to Canon Lane because the Chichester City Band happened to be marching up the street playing a gay tune. ... The band, which was headed by a man with a Union Jack, was really there to advertise the whist drive which is being organised in aid of the National Exchequer funds, but whether Mr Gandhi and his friends realised this or not is problematic. It certainly looked as if they had turned out specially to welcome him.'

Gandhi with Bishop Bell in Chichester.

Gandhi responded graciously, waving to the crowd as the car turned into Canon Lane.

Though private, the weekend was clearly a busy one. A Miss Slade, a Miss Muriel Lester and the Revd C.F. Andrews were also staying at the Bishop's Palace.

It seems likely that the Mahatma was the first to rise on the Sunday morning. The *Observer* records that he was up before 6 a.m. for a walk around Chichester and along the banks of the canal. One can't help wondering about the reaction of anyone staggering home after a heavy night on the tiles. Would they have been believed when they slurred: 'Hey, you'll never guess who I've just seen walking round the canal.'

The Sunday also brought for the Mahatma his trip to Bognor where he visited Mr C.P. Scott, the former editor of the *Manchester Guardian*, who was living at the Lawns, Campbell Road.

But as the *Observer* noted, 'Very few saw Mr Gandhi at Bognor Regis for his visit was kept private.' But what about that goat? Does anyone know? A recent TV programme confirmed that his goat was with him in London on that trip. But did the goat venture into West Sussex?

[25 September 2003]

INDEX

Numbers in **bold** refer to illustration page numbers

A&N, Chichester, 31, 74
Acford's, R.J., 84
Adams, Paul, 146
Adams, Polly, 118-19, **119**
Adsdean House, Funtington,
  20, 21-2, **22**, 54, 55
Alexandra, Princess, 109, **110**
Almodington, 76
Ambrose, Gilbert, 25
Anderson, K.D., 76, 77
Appleby, George, 155-6, **155**
Apuldram, 39, 64
Armadale Road, Chichester,
  35
Arnold, June, 46-7, **46, 47**
Arundel, 9, 109
Ashcroft, Peggy, 110
Assembly Rooms, North
  Street, Chichester, 14, 59,
  60, 114
Atkinson, Ann, 46
Avenue de Chartres, Chich-
  ester, 155
Avenue, The, Chichester, 63
Ayling, Charles, 128-30, **129**
Ayling, Lisa (née Barns), 80

Baker, Bernard, 135
Balchin, 'Boy', 32-3, **33**
Balchin, Joyce, **33**
Balchin, 'Morry', 33
Barnett, Hazel (née Wood),
  54-5
Barnham, 104
Barnham Boys, 88, 89
Bates, Harold Christopher,
  15-16
Bateson, Timothy, 117-18
Beacher, Gary, 86
Bell, Alan, 76-7
Bessborough, Lord, 109
Birdham, 23
Birdham School, 14
Bishop Bell, 83, 157-8, **157**,
  158-60, **160**
Bishop Otter College,
  Chichester, 150
Bishop Otter College School,
  Chichester, 10-12, **11**
Bishop's Palace, Chichester,
  75, 157
Blogg, Eric, **102**
Bognor Regis, 7, 9, 31, 36,
  40, 45, 50, 52, 53, 54, 61,

62, 65, 67, 105, 106, 123,
  146, 158
Bognor Town Band, 100
Bosham, 7, 13, 36, 120, 132,
  144
Bosham Hoe, 145
Bottrill, Robert, 99, 100
Boxall, Joan, **82**
Boxall, Keith, 84-5
Boxgrove, 20
Boys, Jeannette, **101**
Bracklesham, 43
Bracklesham Bay, 83, 84, 130
Bradlaw, Sheila, 46
Brett, Jeremy, 120
Brighton, 70, 96, 106, 107,
  135
Broken Heart, The, 111,
  116, 118
Brown, Liz, 104
Brown, Peter, 104
Broyle, The, Chichester, 36
Bryan, Jan, 103
Burchell, Wyndham, 6-7, **6, 7**
Burden, Frank, 62-4, **63**
Burden, Henry, 63
Burden, Jeremy, **63**, 64
Burgess, Dennis, 151-2
Burke, Pamela (née Harris),
  48-9
Butler, Alf, 66-7, **67**
Butler, Iva, 66-7, **67**
Butler, Jack, **67**
Butlins, Bognor Regis, 87, 88

Cakeham Tower, 43
Cambrai Avenue, Chichester,
  82, 150
Campbell, Malcolm, 96-9, **96**
Campbell, Marilyn, 107-08,
  107
Canal Basin, Chichester, 65
Canon Lane, Chichester,
  159, 160
Cash, Teresa, 146
Central Boys School,
  Chichester, 50-1, **51**, 52,
  84, 124, **124**
Central Girls School, Chich-
  ester, 26, 51, 52, 80
Chances, The, 111, 116, 118,
  121
Chapel Street, Chichester,
  29, 52, 80

Chapman, Vivien, 46
Charlton, 34
Chichester Bookshop, 145
Chichester Boys Club, 81, **86,**
  87, 135, **135**, 136, 151, 152
Chichester Cathedral, 23, 31,
  34, 59, 83
Chichester Cinema at New
  Park, 112
Chichester City Band, 99-100,
  99, **100**, 159
Chichester City Council, 142
Chichester City Football
  Club, 124
Chichester City United, 126
Chichester Crematorium, 145
Chichester Cross, 13, 150,
  159
Chichester District Council,
  87, 155
Chichester District Museum,
  87
Chichester Festival Theatre,
  50, 91, 109-22, **114**, **115**,
  116, **121**
Chichester Folk Song Club,
  107-08, **107**, **108**
Chichester Girls Training
  Corps, **74**
Chichester High School for
  Boys, 50, 52-3, **53**, 76, **77**
Chichester High School for
  Girls, 45
Chichester Judo, 156
Chichester Model Aeroplane
  Society, 156
Chichester Nursery School,
  72, 73
Chichester Players, 156
Chichester Press Ltd, 138
Chichester Society, 156
Chichester Territorials, **15**
Chichester Youth Theatre
  Group, 156
Chidham, 26, 36
Childs, Richard, 134
Chilgrove, 19, 40
Chimes At Midnight, 118
Chitty, Nigel, 55-6
Christ's Hospital, near
  Horsham, 73
Clayton, Clive, 86
Clear, Brian 'Spyder', 82-3
Clemens, Marion, 46, 75

Cleveland Road, Chichester, 84
Coe, Ron, 107
College Lane, Chichester, 11, 72
Compton, 34
Compton, Fay, 109
Congregational Church, South Street, Chichester, 50
Cooper, Joan, 94-5
Corbally, Molly, 154-5
Corkrey, Chalky, **107**
County Hall, Chichester, 7, 31, 146
Covers, Chichester, 10, 64-5, 82
Croucher, Ronald, **102**
Crypt, The, South Street, Chichester, 147

Dadswell, Sylvia (née Halfacree), 152-4
Davis-Poynter, Maureen, 145
Dawe, Jill, **74**
Dawson, Charles, 130-1, **130**
Dell Quay, 36
Dent, John, 145
D'Este Eastes, John, 100-02
Dixon, Brenda, 104
Dixon, Charles, **103**, 104
Dods, Eve, 103
Dolphin and Anchor Hotel, Chichester, 137, 138
Doman, Madeline, 102-4, **103**
Donnington, 76
Down, Alec, **11**
Drake, Sally, 146
Duke of Richmond, 7th, 14
Duke of Richmond, 9th, 58
Duke of Richmond, 10th, 58, 134
Duleepsinhji, 134-5, **134**
Duncton, 153
Dunlop, Enid, 101
Dunlop, Norman, 101
Dutch Courtesan, The, 120

Easebourne, 6
East Dean, 22, 23
Eastgate, Chichester, 142
Eastgate pub, Chichester, 92
East Wittering, 43
El Bolero, South Street, Chichester, 88, 89
Elphick, Michael, 114-15
Esplanade Theatre, Bognor Regis, 89
Evans, Lionel, **41**, 74
Evans, Mary, 40-1, 44
Evershed-Martin, Leslie, 50, 91, 109, **109**, 112, 113, **115**, 121, 122
Exchange cinema, Chichester, 45

Farenden, Amy (née Birch), 10-12, **11**
Felpham, 123, 159
Fido, David, 103

Fielder, Jim, 104
Field's Garage, South Street, Chichester, 47
Finlay, Frank, 109, 115, 119-20, **120**
Fishbourne, 6, 31, 41, 42, 83, 145
Fisher, Arthur, **3**, 3-4, **4**
Fittleworth, 32, 33, 93, 94
Fittleworth School, 33
Fleece, The, Chichester, 98
Fleet, Sydney, 7
Fleming, Helen, 75
Florence Road, Chichester, 60
Flynn, Micky, 135
Fogden, Peggy, **74**
Fontwell, 159
Fontwell racecourse, 98
Ford, 36, 39
43rd Grill, West Street, Chichester, 83
Foster, Judy, 46
Fountain, The, South Street, Chichester, 108
Francis, Sheila, 75-6
Franklin Place, Chichester, 34, **59**, 114, 156
Franks, Terry (née Baldwin), 78
Frederick Hill Ltd, 62, 63, 64
Fuller, Natalie, 71-3, **72**
Funtington, 9, 39, 45
Funtington Players, 100-02, **101, 102**

Gammon, Mike, 104
Gandhi, 157, 158-60, **159, 160**
Garland, Sir Archibald, 13
Garner, Brian, 83-4
Garnett, Ted, 84
Gartside, Bryan, 88-9, **89**
Gaumont cinema, Chichester, 45, 76, 83, 84, 94, 95, **95**, 96
Georgiades, Geoff, 145
Gick, Tricia, 145
Gillingham, Elizabeth, 26
Gillingham, John, 26
Gillingham, Leslie, 26-7, **26**
Gillingham, Wilfred, 26
Ginman, Heather, 51-2
Glaister, Eddie, 140
Goodman, David, 109
Goodwood, 23, 27, 34, 58, 60, 122
Gough, Mary, 46
Grainger, Dennis, 50-1
Granada cinema, Chichester, 76, 84, 96-9, **96, 97, 98**
Graylingwell Hospital, Chichester, 13, 47, 52, 147, 148
Green, Ken, 147
Green Lane, Chichester, 142
Green, Tim, 86
Greenshields, Archie, 60-2, **61, 62**, 105-6, **105, 106**
Greenslade, Molly, 7
Greenwood, Joan, 109
Gribble, The, Oving, 108

Griffiths, Richard, 146
Grove Road, Chichester, 4

Haigh, Graham, **82**
Halford, Edward, **101**
Hall, Kathleen, 7
Hall, Margaret, 46
Hambrook, 27, 28
Handyman, The, 119
Hardwicke, Edward, 120
Harris, Charles, 17-18, **17**, **18**
Harris, Dorothy, 18, 20-1, **20**
Harris, Vivian, 49-50, **50**
Harting, 73
Haskins, Jane (née Clayton), 80
Haslett, Ian, 7
Haylor, Margaret, 59-60, **59**
Heath, Sir Edward, 41-2, **42**
Hellyer, Frank, 64-5, **65**
Hendry's, Chichester, 137
Henfrey, Janet, 116-17
Hide, Lenny, 125
Highfield Lane, Oving, 18
Hill, Harold, 35
Hill, John, 35-6
Hill, Muriel, 35-6
Hoad, Vera, 147-9, **148, 149**
Hole, Everil, 71
Hole In The Wall, The, 86, 107, 108
Holland, Kevin, 145
Holt, Janet, 23
Hood, Jack, 135
Hornet, The, Chichester, 64, 65, 141, 142, 145
Horsham, 150
Hove, 133, 134, 150
Howick, Molly, **125**
Howick, Peter, 124-5
Howick, Ronald, 124-5, **124**, **125**
Hughes, Peter, 73-4
Hutton, Ian, 37-8

Ifould, Andy, 87-8, **88**
Inlands Farm, Nutbourne, **28**
It Can Damage Your Health, 115
Itchenor, 119
Ivanhoe cricket club, 125

Jacobi, Derek, 109, 115, 120, **121, 122**
James, Edward, 140
Joice, Mary (née Balmer), 158
Jones, Peter, 88
Jubilee Gardens, Chichester, 142

Kaye, Danny, 122
Keith, Penelope, **116**
Kidd, Surgeon-Colonel, 13, 47
Kimbell's, Chichester, 95
King, Barbara, 46
King, Gladys, 47-8
Kingley Vale, 9
Kingsham School, 78
Kings Theatre, Southsea, 90, 93

Knights, Edith, 9-10, **9**, **10**, 21-2, **22**
Knights, Walter, 22, **22**

Lagness, 39
Lancastrian School, Chichester, 31-2, **31**, 81, 84, 85, 87, 114, 135
Lavant, 80, 136
Lavant Church, 21
Lawlor, Steve, 146
Leconfield House, Petworth, 33
Lee, Iris, 7
Lee, Thelma, 7
Leggett, Dorothy Rose, **21**
Leggett, Freda, 17-18, **18**, 20-1, **20**, **21**
Leggett, George, **18**, **20**, **21**
Leigh Road, Chichester, **68**
Leveson-Gower, the Rev F.A.G., **13**
Lewis, James, **101**
Lewis Road, Chichester, 65
Lewis, Roy, 85
Liberator crash, Chichester, 35, 39, 40, **40**, 53, 65, 81, 82
Lime Close, Chichester, 151
Lion Street, Chichester, 59
Litten, The, Chichester, 142
Littlehampton, 8, 9, 61, 63, 78
Little London, Chichester, 35
Lodge Hill, near Pulborough, 89, 90
Lomas, Peter, 155
Long, Arch, 22-3
Long, Kenneth, 39, 64, 65
Longhurst, Doreen, 46
Loot, 115
Love For Love, **122**
Ludlow, Gillian, 46
Luke, Jack, **68**
Lyddall, Herbert, 1-2
Lyddall, James, 1-2, **2**

Manhood School, 75
Mann, Dick, 107
Mansbridge, Freddie, 18-19, **19**
Market Avenue, Chichester, 71
Marks and Spencer's, Chichester, 24
Marmont, Sue, 75
Marriner, Joan (née Burchell), 6-7
Maslen, George, 125-6
Mason's Garage, Southgate, Chichester, 57
Matson, Ruth, 46
Matthews, Wendy, 84
Meaker, Paddy, 46
Melbourne Road, Chichester, 3
Mellor, F.R.S., 147
Mellor, G., 147
Merston, 4, 39
Michell, Keith, 109, **116**

Midhurst, 6, 46, 47, 93, 94
Milanes, Rosamond, 7-8
Miller, Jack, 57-8, **57**, **58**
Miller, John, 57, 58
Miller's Motor School, 58
Mills, Lillian, 145
Mitchell, Alfred, 29-30, **30**
Mitchell, Margaret, 29, 30, **30**
Monsieur Amilcar, **116**
Moore, Bobby, 128
Morey, Richard, 23
Morris, Paul, 107
Mountbatten, Louis, 1st Earl Mountbatten of Burma, 20, 21-2, 54
Munro, Charles, 135-136, **135**

Neville, John, 111
Newbury, Ken, 141, 151
Newell Centre, St Pancras, Chichester, 137
Newlands Lane, Chichester, 128
New Park Centre, Chichester, 84, 155-6, **155**
New Park Playgroup, 156
New Park Road, Chichester, 141, 142, **142**, 156
Nieman, Michael, 52-4, **53**
Norris, Eileen, 110-12, **111**
Northchapel, 25
Northgate, Chichester, 63, 142
North Mundham, 55, 56
North Street, Chichester, 31, 58
Nutbourne post office, 26
Nye, Jack, 132-3, **132**, **133**

Oaklands Park, Chichester, 110, 118, 128
Object, The, 85-7, **85**
O'Connell, Ruth, 144
Odeon cinema, Chichester, 21, 45, 76, 84, **95**
O'Gorman, Brian, 104-05
O'Gorman, Dave, 104
O'Gorman, Joe, 104-05
Old Theatre Royal, Portsmouth, 90
Oliver Whitby Road, Chichester, 39
Oliver Whitby School, Chichester, 73-4
Olivier, Laurence, 91, 109, 110, 111, 112, 113, **113**, 114, 115, **115**, 116, 117, 118, 119, 120
O'Neill, Martin, 143
Orchard Street, Chichester, 52, 59, 66, 155
Othello, 109, 112, 113

Pagham, 9, 50, 68
Pagham Harbour, 37
Pailthorpe, Richard, 23
Parklands, Chichester, 68
Parsons, Angie, 92, **92**
Peacheries, The, Bognor Road,

Chichester, 40, 74
Pearce, Jane, 45-6
Perrott, Cyril, 31-2, **31**
Petherbridge, Edward, 120
Petworth, 32, 61, 106
Petworth Boys School, 32-3
Petworth Engineering Company, 32
Petworth police pantomime, **62**
Plant, Geoffrey, **101**
Plowright, Joan, 109, **113**, 115, 119, 120
Porter, Roy, 157-8
Portfield Football Club, 124, 125, 126
Portfield Hall, Chichester, 71
Portfield Sunday School, Chichester, 71
Portsmouth, 34, 35, 36, 39, 44, 47, 57, 65, 67, 68, 93, 110, 135, 153
Preston, Arthur, 136
Price, Bernard, 147
Prichard, Dorothy, 96
Prime, Heinz, 55, 56
Priory Park, Chichester, 80, 123

Quarry Lane, Chichester, 65
Queen Elizabeth II, 150, **151**
Queen Elizabeth the Queen Mother, **121**

Ranjitsinhji, 134
Redgrave, Michael, 109
Rex Ballroom, Bognor Regis, 89
Richards, Keith, 88
River Lavant, 66, 141-2
Robinson, Jane, 143-4
Rogate, 4
Rogers, Pieter, 110, 111, 112, 113, 117
Rose Green, 50, 68
Rossington, Norman, 120
Roussillon Barracks, Chichester, 50, 70
Rowes Hornets cricket club, 125
Royal Close, Chichester, 71
Royal Sussex Regiment, 1, 2, 4, 50
Royal West Sussex Hospital, Chichester, 55, **152**, 154-5
Rugg, Miggy, **107**
Russell, Tony, 85-7
Rustington, 61, 106

Sainsbury's fire, Chichester, 137, **139**
Saint Joan, 113, 115, 120
St Andrew's Church, West Dean, 140
St Cyriac's, Chichester, 80
St Faith's, Chichester, 147
St George's Church, Whyke, Chichester, **91**
St George's Hall, Whyke, Chichester, 87

St James' School, Chichester, 35
St Martin's Street, Chichester, 31, 138
St Pancras, Chichester, 36, 142, 147
St Pancras Church, Chichester, 146
St Paul's Church, Chichester, **125**
St Paul's Road, Chichester, 96
St Paul's youth club, Broyle Road, Chichester, 50
St Richard's Hospital, Chichester, 84, 147, 152-4, **153**,
Saturday, Sunday ... And Monday, 116
Saunders, William, 126-7, **127**
Sayers, Fittleworth, 33
Scicluna, Anne, 82-3, **82, 83**
Scott, C.P., **159**, 160
Scott, Gary, 144
Seafare fish restaurant, Northgate, Chichester, 98
Seal Club, Earnley, 135
Seaman, Pat, 45
Sears, Margaret, 7
Selsey, 8, 9, 14, 23, 24, 37, 39, 97, 120
Selsey Secondary Modern School, 76
Sergio's, St Martin's Street, Chichester, 88
Servant of Two Masters, A, 122
Shackleton, Amy Vibert, 147
Shackleton, Francis Richard, 147
Shamrock Close, Chichester, 128
Shearing, Bernard, 7
Shepperd, Sheila, 104
Shippam, Bassil, 135
Shippam's, 4, 6
Shirley's, North Street, Chichester, 137
Shopwhyke, 34
Sidlesham, 76, 78
Sidlesham Football Club, 75
Singleton, **12, 13**, 144, 145
Slaughter, Arthur, 23-4, **24**
Slaughter, Jeanne, 23-5, **24**
Slaughter, Jimmy, 23
Slindon, 34, 103, 104
Slingo, Charles, 39-40, **39**
Sluggett, Julian, 89-91, **90, 91**
Smith, Cicely (née Dance), 123
Smith, Maggie, 109, 120
Smith, Teddy, 109
Smuts, Esme, 41, 42
Southbourne, 89
Southgate, Chichester, 100
South Mundham, 36, 37
South Pallant, Chichester, 66
South Street, Chichester, **79**, 89, 150

Spencer, Arthur, 104
Spershott, James, 142
Stenning, Roy, 69-70, **69, 70**
Stephens, Robert, 115, 120
Stephenson, Jacqueline, 46
Stockbridge Road, Chichester, 57
Stone, Joan, 7
Stone, Marcia, 7
Stoughton, **145**
Stride, John, 120
Stubbs, Arthur, 47, 48
Stubbs, Joan, 48
Stubbs, Kate, 47, 48
Sussex County Cricket Club, 132-3, 134-5
Swan, H.J., 13

Tadd, Edward, 99, 100, **100**
Tadd, Eric, 99-100, **99**
Tangmere, 34, 36, 37, 39, 45, 87
Tennant, A.H., 21
Tennent, Duncan, 15-16
Terminus Road, Chichester, 138
Tester, Barry, 81-2
Tester, Hilda, **29**, 30
Tester, Vera, 29, 30
Thair, David, 145
Thatcher, Ron, 32-4, **32**
Theobald, Myra, 43, **44**
Theobald, Neil, 43-4, **44**
Thomas, Madeline, 25
Thomas, Taffy, 84
Thorndike, Sybil, 109, 112, 116
Thorney Island, 36, 37, 38, 39
Tucker, Stefan, 136
Tulett, Charles, 4-6, **4, 5, 6**
Tulett, Victor, 6
Turnbull, Alderman, 13
Turner, Dave, 50-1, **51**
Turpin, Randy, **135**
Twine, Winifred, 26, **26**
Tyndale-Biscoe, Arthur, 7-9, **8**

Uncle Vanya, 112, 120
Upwaltham, 23
Ustinov, Peter, 99

Valente, Vic, 93-4
Vick, Grahame, 85-7, **86, 87**
Vivash, Harold, 65-6
Voller, Audrey, 128, **128**

Wakeford, Harry, 27-8, **27**
Wakeford, Maggie, 27-8
Walberton Choral Group, 102
Walberton Village Hall, 103
Walberton WI, 103
Walton, Mabel (née Paine), 59, **59**
Walton, William, 59-60, **60**
Watkins, Dorothy, 38-9, **38**
Weald and Downland Museum, Singleton, 23

Webb, Erica (née Eyles), 78
Weller, Johnny, 135
Weller, Sam, **64**
Wells, Stanley, 34
West Ashling, 21, 100
West Ashling School, 10, **10**
Westbourne, 25
West Dean, 37, 140
Westgate, Chichester, 65, 66
Westhampnett, 39
Westhampnett cemetery (now Portfield), 149
West Lavant, 17
Westloats Lane School, 123
West Stoke, 18
West Street, Chichester, 47, 59, 73
West Sussex County Council, 86, 89
West Sussex County Record Office, 134
West Sussex Football League, 126
West Wittering, 15, 43, 48, 49
West Wittering Parochial School, **44**
Wheeler, Spokey, **107**
Whitbourn, Jeanne, 150
White, Brian, 135, **135**, 136
White, Johnny, 135
White, Paul, 137-138
Whitelaw, Billie, 120
Whyke housing estate, Chichester, **157**
Whyke Infants School, Chichester, 84
Willard Developments, Chichester, 68
Willard Electrical, Chichester, 68
Willard, Gladys, 3-4
Willard, Herbert, 67, **68**
Willard, Jack, 68-9, **68**
Willis, Audrey (née Evans), 74-5, **74, 75**
Winslow Boy, The, 118
Witterings, 44, 63, 76, 88, 144
WOADS (Walberton Operatic and Amateur Dramatic Society), 102-04, **103**
Woodlands Children's Home, Chichester, **72**
Woolpack Inn, 41
Workhouse Donkey, The, 113, 120
World Stores, Chichester, 24
Worthing, 59, 61, 76, 106, 133, 150
Wyatt, Annie, 38-9, **39**
Wyatt, Frank, 38
Wyatt, Gordon, 38
Wyatt, Jack, **39**
Wyatt, John, 38
Wyatt, Roger, 38
Wyatt, Ron, 38
Wyatt, Tom, 38
Wyatt, William, 38